SPIRIT
ROADS

SPIRIT ROADS

AN EXPLORATION OF
OTHERWORLDLY ROUTES

PAUL DEVEREUX

COLLINS & BROWN

© Vega 2003
Text © Paul Devereux 2003

First published in 2003 by Vega
This issue published in 2007 by
Collins & Brown
151 Freston Road
London
W10 6TH

An imprint of Anova Books Company Ltd

Distributed in the United States and Canada by
Sterling Publishing Co, 387 Park Avenue South, New York, NY 10016, USA

The moral right of the author has been asserted.

ISBN: 9 78184 340 406 4

A CIP catalogue record for this book is available from the British Library.

10 9 8 7 6 5 4 3 2 1

Printed and bound by Creative Print and Design, Ebbw Vale, Wales

This book can be ordered direct from the publisher.
Contact the marketing department, but try your bookshop first.

www.anovabooks.com

CONTENTS

ACKNOWLEDGEMENTS

I owe an enormous debt of gratitude to traditional storyteller, author, and folklorist Eddie Lenihan of Clare, Ireland, for providing me with so much information and insight, not to mention his valued companionship on field trips in Clare and Kerry. I am similarly indebted to author, storyteller, teacher, musician, and folklorist Bob Curran of Northern Ireland for his tremendous help and for his delightful company during a field trip in and around Fermanagh. I am further grateful to Frank Olding of Wales for going out of his way to provide me with key information, to William Folan of Campeche, Mexico, for finding time out of his busy field research and university schedules to talk with me, and to Harry Casey of California for helpful discussions. And without the years of research by John Palmer in the Netherlands and Ulrich Magin in Germany there would have been little to write about regarding Otherworldly routes in those countries. The similar work of Laurence Main in Wales is also noteworthy. The research of many others is recorded in the reference section.

It has been a delight meeting so many friendly and helpful people during the fieldwork for this book. I thank them all, whether met in rural homes, country pubs, or highways and byways, and my gratitude is not diminished because they are anonymous to me. However, I do have the names of the following people to whom I am grateful for special kindnesses, information, and other help: in England – Margaret Bunney and her colleagues at Ludgvan Church, and John Drinkwater at Swindale Head; in Ireland – Francis Carson and his mother Kathleen at Moneygashel, John Codd of Kilcowan, the Curtin family in Kerry, Mick O'Dwyer of Drumline, Margaret Gallagher of the Belcoo and District Historical Society, Sean Haran of Cloonagh, Mayo, Timmy Scanlon of Kerry, and Jimmy Walsh in Clare.

I was greatly assisted by staff at certain reference libraries. First and foremost my gratitude goes to Deirdre Hennigan and Bairbre Ni Fhloinn of the Department of Irish Folklore at University College Dublin for their help and patience. I also thank Michael Dempsey at Wexford Public Library, and the staffs in the map sections of Truro Museum, and in Leicester reference library. Various people have helped me with information that proved useful in the writing of this book, whether in the form of passing on literature and newspaper snippets to me, or for providing me with personal introductions. Among their number are: Stuart Booth, David Clarke, Barbara Crocker, Marion Grooms, Jeremy Harte, Rose Heaword, Neil Mortimer, Bob

Trubshaw, Damian Walter, and Sybil Webster. Other sources are cited in the text. I also wish to thank Neil Mortimer, editor of *3rd Stone,* for allowing me to use two of my articles for his journal as foundations for Chapters Two and Three of this book.

My wife, Charla Devereux, accompanied me on field trips in England, Wales, Ireland, and the United States, and my son, Sol Devereux, came with me on various US and Mexican expeditions, and conducted research for me on an English location. Quite apart from their excellent company, I would not have got through all that fieldwork without their help.

None of the people mentioned above are to be held in any way responsible for any errors that may have crept into this volume through my own ineptitude.

Finally, I gratefully acknowledge the generosity of The Lifebridge Foundation, New York, for funding some of my fieldwork in the Americas, and the International Consciousness Research Laboratories (ICRL), Princeton, for funding some of the Irish fairy path field research.

Photographs
All the photographs in this book are by the author, except where credit is otherwise given in the captions.

INTRODUCTION

Ways Less Travelled

Today we rarely think about roads as being anything other than mundane features, usually travelled by motor vehicles, that connect one place with another. It was not always like this. In the pre-modern world, as far back as we can detect, there were ordinary, everyday roads and tracks and there were other special routes that had symbolic, ceremonial, spiritual or magical attributes – and sometimes all these properties combined. Even the meeting and parting of ways, what we dismiss as "crossroads" or "intersections", were regarded as being important locations freighted with supernatural significance. This book looks at these special types of route – paths, tracks and roads – that tend to be less travelled these days. Even where these routes are still in service their function has changed and most of the people that use them now do not know about their original significance.

In Part One, a series of chapters presents background information on a range of routes displaying various "Otherworldly" qualities. These include Australian Aboriginal dreaming tracks (also known as "songlines"), fairy paths and other spirit ways of various kinds, corpse roads, mysterious ritual and ceremonial roads in the Americas, and Stone-Age linear features that may well have been seen as spirit roads by their builders and users. In the process of presenting these concise overviews, various fresh insights emerge in regard to the "secret histories" of certain features, and the possible former existence of an archaic common spiritual geography spanning the whole of the Asian and European continents.

In Part Two, a Sampler offers a close-up look at these various routes by presenting a selection of examples from various countries along with specific geographical information about them. As far as I am aware, there has never before been such a comprehensive attempt to physically ground the "psychogeographies" of antiquity.

The Sampler
The Sampler contains fifty-five examples of all the various kinds of Otherworldly route mentioned above. There could, of course, have been thousands of examples from the countries featured and from a great many

more lands besides. For purely practical reasons of time, resources, and the extent of this book it is possible to present only a token sample. Nevertheless, that is sufficient to cover many types of special route, giving a detailed insight into their nature.

Many, even most, of the entries in the Sampler describe routes that the reader can visit if so interested and able to do so, either in his or her own country or when visiting any of the other lands included, and information is provided in each entry's description to help with this. (There are some examples listed, though, that are not suitable or appropriate for visiting, and this becomes clear in the entries concerned.) I hope the reader uses the Sampler in this way. However, its *prime* purpose is to present a detailed picture of Otherworldly routes, to provide the reader with information about what they are really like and the lore and other details of interest attributed to them that only specific case descriptions can provide. In short, the Sampler is designed to put flesh on the bones of the overviews in Part One. It is meant to be read, and its use as a field guide should be thought of as a secondary function, a bonus. In both these functions, it is hoped that the Sampler will help alert the reader to a land-based spiritual legacy, a conceptual heritage that is rapidly disappearing or, more accurately in some cases, is becoming invisible to the modern mind.

Fieldwork
Considerable fieldwork was undertaken specially for this book, but some has been carried out in the course of my general research over several years. It is clear in the Sampler that I have focused mainly on Britain and Ireland, as these are my native landscapes and in any case they happen to furnish a good range of route examples, but I am familiar with all the other landscapes included in the sample (with the exception of Costa Rica), and in particular have conducted considerable exploration of enigmatic roads and tracks in Mexico and the United States.

A special word should be said about the Irish fairy paths that account for eleven entries in the Sampler, a fifth of the total sample. Several long field trips in Ireland were required for this work, in two of which I was greatly aided by the Irish field folklorist Eddie Lenihan and in one by folk expert Bob Curran. The fieldwork was also based on preliminary literature research, especially in the remarkable Irish Folklore Commission archives in the Department of Irish Folklore at University College Dublin. The main bulk of this material was assembled by full-time collectors working for the Commission, each familiar with the dialect and lore of their respective districts, as well as by many part-time and specialist collectors. A large proportion of the archive material consists of verbatim transcripts of field recordings made on Ediphone machines and in later years on tape-recorders. In 1937-38 much folklore was brought in by the "Schools' Scheme" in which schoolchildren throughout most of Ireland obtained lore from family members and friends using specially-prepared guidelines. In total, these archives form a formidable body of data, much of it handwritten, and some of it in Gaelic. It represents a kind of memory bank of oral lore handed down from generation to generation – a process now rapidly in decline.

Even with access to all these various sources, the finding and geographical plotting of fairy paths proved to be a huge problem. Fairy paths were rarely if ever fully described by folklore sources, and unlike the humorous sign shown in the photograph on the back jacket of this book, there are no signposts pointing out the courses of these invisible features. Much detective work was required, and it is a fact that more instances were investigated in the field without success than found their way into the Sampler. Apart from the difficulty caused by the vague nature of the references to the course of fairy paths in the available lore, the vast bulk of what information there is came from people now deceased. More than once we had whole neighbourhoods out trying to help us identify specific houses that had been said to be on fairy paths, and it usually ended up with us all scratching our heads in befuddlement. The reason was easy to understand: elderly people providing lore in, say, the 1930s, were themselves referring to information they received in their youth, sometimes from people who were elderly then. So our fieldwork in Ireland frequently consisted of trying to pin down information originating a century or more ago. I came to the conclusion that as far as fairy paths were concerned I was writing this book a decade or two too late. So it is that the Sampler can offer no descriptions of magically glittering spirit highways hovering over the Irish countryside, commencing at clearly defined locations and ending at equally certain destinations; rather, it contains information on a few rare fragments. The Sampler provides real, raw information, not fanciful confectionery.

Ontology

Finally, I must address a frequently asked question: do I actually believe in fairies and ghosts and spirits, or am I just treating the material simply as folklore? Well, it *is* folklore, and by and large that is how I handle it. It is folklore-in-the-landscape, lore with geographical corollaries of one kind or another. We are dealing with what has been termed a "cognised landscape" whether we are considering fairy paths in Ireland, songlines in Australia, ritual roads in the Americas, or death roads in Europe. They all represent the mapping of mindscapes that were projected onto the physical landscape in past times. Indeed, one of the reasons for conducting research into such features is to gain a glimpse of worldviews that existed long before our modern culture, for it is always a good idea to look at our world from different angles lest we slip into the dangerous belief that our present worldview is the only true one.

Even though my interest in the kind of material contained within this volume is primarily of a folkloric, archaeological and anthropological nature, it does not mean that I think there are no strange, Otherworldly aspects to the land. I suspect that there were probably mysterious sightings and experiences that formed the specks of grit around which the pearls of lore and belief grew. The reason I think this is because of my own experiences. I remember one summer twilight seeing totally inexplicable yellow-white luminous orbs flickering on treetops at the foot of the Brecon Beacons in Wales, and one warm night-time peering into a small, arid, and utterly remote valley in the Kimberley region of Australia to observe small, soft-blue lights playing around beneath our vantage point. I further recall an overcast late afternoon in Ireland when my wife and I were driving along a lonely country lane: our attention was simultaneously caught by a "something" that materialized on a broad grass verge to our left. It stood about 3 ft (90 cm) in height and was vaguely anthropomorphic, but there were no details. It looked like one of those densely and repetitively patterned pictures that reveal a three-dimensional image if looked at in a certain way. In this case the thing was a discreet, three-dimensional form that seemed to visually emerge from the texture of a bank of foliage that was many feet behind it. And then it was gone. We were convinced that we had seen something objective, however strange and fleeting it may have been, because we both caught sight of it out of the corners of our eyes at the same moment. All these sightings were in landscapes selected in the Sampler, and all would fit the description of "spirits" in one form or another. And I have witnessed other, equally odd phenomena, so I would not be so arrogant as to claim that we know absolutely everything about the natural landscapes that surround us. It is just that today most of the human race is removed from such natural environments by urban development. And due to the way we now travel, our artificial lighting that brightens the night, and the culture we dwell in, we rarely if ever see anything strange – though reports of spectral happenings in the great outdoors do still come in from drivers travelling along lonely highways at night.[1] But if we were to spend long periods of time far from city lights in mountains, deserts or forests, especially if in the company of people of a cultural background that allowed spirits into its worldview, our experiences might be very different. Many anthropologists, mountaineers, desert walkers and lone seafarers have tales to tell of seeing inexplicable phenomena. I know one anthropologist who lived for a long time with a rainforest Indian tribe, and he eventually began to see and experience things that back in his own European culture would have been viewed as impossible or paranormal. Any worldview is very dependent on the cultural context to which it belongs, which makes reality a moveable feast.

Paul Devereux

GLOSSARY

A small number of specialist words and terms will be used in this book that may be unfamiliar or unclear to some readers, and it is hoped this short list may be of assistance where this is the case.

bier	Framework or cart for carrying a corpse, either in a coffin or in a canvas bag.
bridleway	Pathway used by horse-riders. Usually wider and better defined than a footpath.
bullroarer	Aerodynamic wooden object that issues a whistling or humming sound when swung rapidly around on a string.
cairn	Heap or mound made up of small rocks.
cup-markings	Artificially-carved round hollows usually appearing with other markings in prehistoric rock art.
hamlet	A group of buildings too small to comprise a village.
henge	Neolithic monument comprising a circular area defined by a ditch and outer bank.
hollow road	Track sunk between pronounced earthen banks, usually dating from the Medieval period. Also known as a "sunken road".
megalith	Literally large ("mega") stone ("lith"). Megalithic monuments are therefore those built from large stones. The term is usually applied to structures belonging to the Neolithic era of prehistory.
metalled road	Hard-surfaced road, usually with tarmac or concrete.
motte and bailey	Remnant of a Norman (Medieval era) castle mound (the motte) surrounded by a defensive earthwork (the bailey).
necromancy	Divination by means of communication with the dead.
sacbe (pl. *-ob)*	Mayan term meaning "white way" referring to ancient Mayan causeways.
shamanism	Trance-based system of divination, healing and spirituality. The shaman would use any of a number of methods for entering trance (drumming, chanting, dancing, using mind-altering drugs, etc.), in which he or she would experience "spirit flight", an ecstatic or out-of-body journey to the spirit world (often accompanied by animal spirit helpers). One of the earliest religious

expressions, shamanism typically belonged to tribal societies, though more sophisticated versions of it also occurred in structured societies too. The shaman might visit the spirit world to gain supernatural power, to guide the souls of dying tribal members, to rescue the souls of sick people, to divine the future, to communicate with spiritual beings, or to conduct magical battles with enemy shamans and sorcerers. The shaman was healer, priest, conjuror, trickster, magician, entertainer, tribal historian, and storyteller. Versions of shamanism can be found in many parts of the world ("shamanisms"), the ecstatic state being a universal feature of human consciousness, but "classic" shamanism belongs to central Asia. Shamanism still survives in some cultures around the world.

soakage Australian term for a spring or water seepage in desert country.

stela (pl. -ae) Inscribed or carved upright slab or pillar.

stranded track Poorly defined track in open country; specifically, the route of a track that has developed into more than one parallel course.

tor Natural, often heavily eroded, rock summit of a hill. Sometimes applied to a distinctive, solitary hill.

totem Animal or natural object that is adopted as a symbol of ancestral significance by groups within tribal societies. Hence "totemism", "totemic".

unfenced road Road without fences or hedgerows and so open to the landscape around it.

CHRONOLOGICAL GUIDE

Various terms for generalized periods of history and prehistory are also used throughout the book, and so a simplified chronology is presented here. It is a guide only, not an exact chronology.

Neolithic   *c.*4000 – *c.*2000 BC

Bronze Age   *c.*2000 – *c.* 800 BC

Iron Age   *c.*800 BC – historical era

Romano-British   AD 71 – *c.*410 – period of Roman occupation
                       of Britain

Anglo-Saxon   *c.*AD 400 – 1000

Medieval   *c.*AD 1000 – 1550

Early Modern   *c.*AD 1550 – 1800

Modern   *c.*AD 1800 – present day

PART ONE

BACKGR⊕UND

Overviewing Otherworldly Routes

CHAPTER ONE

Songlines: Tracks of the Dreamtime

Of all the types of Otherworldly routes, the so-called "songlines" of the Australian Aborigines are probably among the ones that most people today are likely to have heard of. These mythological routes relate to the "Dreamtime", a term coined by anthropologists in 1927 for the Aboriginal concept of a magical primordial era that is also perennial, like another dimension to everyday reality. Aborigines themselves call this mythic, timeless time *tjukuba, altjurunga, altjira,* and *dzjugur* among numerous other terms, depending on the tribal language.

Dreamtime Beings

In the Dreamtime dawn, the Earth was a stark, empty place and the land was mainly a monotonous flat, endless plain punctuated only by a few hills and mountains. Then, at some point in that primordial epoch, beings emerged from below the ground – or, in some Aboriginal traditions, from the sky – and started to walk the land. These beings took various forms, though essentially falling into three types: non-human "creatures", and "heroes" with human characteristics or human-animal attributes – the ancestral animal beings. Some were of gigantic stature, or, more often, of size-shifting nature – so in Sampler entry 47, for instance, the Dreamtime heroes can walk through a mountain range creating a gorge, yet later be killed by a pack of wild dogs.

In the course of their travels these Dreamtime beings created the topography of the landscape we see today. They journeyed on routes special to them, along which they camped, made fire, conducted ceremonies, defecated, dug for water, fought, copulated, and so on. All their activities left their marks on the country that can still be seen to this day. A cave mouth is a grieving Dreamtime mother, a distinctive hilltop the cranium of a giant hero embedded in the ground, a creek the line gouged by a Dreamtime being's boomerang or bullroarer, the gaunt branch of a dead tree an Ancestor pointing, a boulder the faeces of a Dreamtime entity, and so forth. Aborigines know and see these things as topographic features just as non-Aborigines see them, but they do so through a kind of mythic filter.

The Dreamtime heroes also sang – they sang their names and of the things they saw and did and felt. When these creator beings finished their journeys, they turned into rocks, trees or other features, or else re-entered the ground.

The Tracks

These routes are variously known by non-Aborigines as "songlines", "dream journey routes" or "dreaming tracks". The last two terms are perhaps more accurately descriptive than the first, which owes its wide currency to a best-selling book by the late Bruce Chatwin.[1] "Songlines" is a bit misleading, as the singing was only one part of a complex of myth and ritual – what the Walbiri refer to as *Gadjari* when talking to non-Aborigines. "Meaning attached to landscape unfolds in language, names, stories, myths and rituals, " Miriam Kahn has observed with regard to the Aboriginals of Papua New Guinea.[2] The "Dreaming" of a particular Dreamtime ancestor is the body of lore and ritual associated with it, including its primordial route through the land, which is like the hanger for the coat of its myth, a topographic mnemonic, a thread of transpersonal memory wending its way across the land. The Yolngu of Arnhemland refer to dreaming tracks as *djalkiri* – "footprints of the ancestors"[3] – and that is perhaps the best definition we can arrive at in English.

"Big Places"

Each of the important sacred or totemic places along a dreaming track had its song, its story, its dance, its body decoration patterns, its ritual. There would once also have been *tjurungas* – ritual objects of stone, wood or bark – secreted at them. A *tjurunga* would be marked with motifs that, in effect, would be a map of that part of the invisible track. It could also indicate the story of the Dreamtime events associated with the site and tell the initiated elder what songs and dances were associated with that spot. In the 1940s, the anthropologist, T G H Strehlow, wrote about a visit to a sacred site – a "Big Place" – in the western MacDonnell Ranges that he made in the company of Aranda tribesmen. He saw an elder take out a bundle of *tjurungas* hidden away in a cleft between boulders. By looking at each of them, the old Aborigine could chant the site's myth depicted on them.[4]

The understanding that the boundaries of Aboriginal tribal territories could be determined by whether or not the elders of a given tribe knew the rituals and songs associated with Big Places on dreaming tracks only became properly understood by non-Aborigines due to the discoveries of anthropologist Charles Mountford. In nearly two decades of ethnological travelling over the central regions of Australia he found that he kept encountering certain myths, which he came to realize had a linear geographical distribution over large distances. In the 1960s he was taken along one of these lines of myths by tribal elders and allowed a deep insight into its nature. This dreaming track and the story of Mountford's important journey along it is described in Sampler entry 46.

Networks of Knowledge

For untold generations Aborigines have followed the dreaming tracks in their territories. Australian poet and author James Cowan points out that with the dreaming tracks "we are not just dealing with an unending journey back and forth across tribal territory . . . Instead we are looking at a sacred journey in which each stage is imbued with sacred significance".[5] Hills, ridges, trees, waterholes, rocks, caves – these are not mere topography but, to the Aborigine, also a real and present spiritual, mythic landscape, and specific landscape features are especially charged with *djang* or numinous power.

The knowledge and ceremonial regard of dreaming tracks still exists in some of the more remote parts of Australia, but now, inevitably, in a more fragmented manner than in former times. Both Gary Snyder and Bruce Chatwin reported witnessing Aborigines gabbling stories to themselves as they were being driven in the bush in four-wheel-drive vehicles. It turned out that they were crossing dreaming tracks or passing Big Places on them. But "dreaming" was meant to be undertaken at walking pace – not while rolling by on wheels at high speed – so the stories had to be told at an unseemly pace.[6]

Knowledge of dreaming tracks can impart important geographical information to the Aborigine, as they link one area with another, and one sacred, totemic site to another. Helen Watson, from her work with Yolngu Aborigines, calls this a "knowledge network", and each person is responsible through singing, dancing and painting for its maintenance. "For Yolngu, what provides the connections between places . . . are the tracks of the Ancestral Beings, and the tracks *are* the landscape, " she writes. "Orientation in space is of prime concern for Yolngu. Any recounting, whether ancestral, historical or contemporary, is framed by a discussion of place: where events happened." [7]

Many non-Aboriginal observers have long commented on the Aborigines' exceptional sense of direction and location. One of these observers, David Lewis, travelled with Aborigines in the Simpson and Western Desert areas between 1972 and 1974, and he witnessed many instances of the Aborigines' highly developed sense of location. He noted that "the main references of the Aborigines proved to be the meandering tracks of the ancestral Dreamtime beings that form a network over the whole Western Desert". When his guides worked out directions for distant non-sacred places the greatest errors (up to 67 per cent) occurred, but when they were using sacred sites as their indicators this fell to a very low error rate (an average of less than 3 per cent). Lewis came to learn that when an Aboriginal looks at a stretch of country "he generally incorporates its mythical with its physical features".

In one particular instance, Lewis witnessed "faultless orientation by the most unobtrusive landmarks" by Pintupi Aborigines. The destination they were aiming for was Tjulyurnya, near a deposit of sacred yellow stones that marked where dingoes drove two Lizard Men underground during the Dreamtime. The Pintupi wished to take some of these stones back to their home, almost three hundred miles (480 km) away. From a place called Yunala, they travelled cross-country for 27 miles (43.5 km) via Namarunya Soak, a tiny hollow that, to Lewis's eyes, "had no identifying features at all"; a site where sharp flints used for knives were found; Rungkaratjunku, a sacred sandhill, and finally to Tjulyurnya, a rock-hole by a small hill at the end of a creek – the actual deposit of yellow stones was in fact over 1 mile (1.5 km) further on from that. "The Pintupi's route-finding by these unremarkable landmarks was uncannily accurate, " Lewis writes. "They always knew just where they were, they knew the direction of spiritually important places for hundreds of kilometres around, and were oriented in compass terms." [8]

Apart from Aborigines' use of the dreaming tracks for religious, ceremonial, social and navigational purposes, there are also persistent, ages-old rumours that their *karadji* – magician-shamans sometimes referred to as "Clever Men" or "Men of High Degree" – can (or once could) pass information telepathically along them.[9] Information received in this way can apparently vary from moods and feelings to full-blown visions.[10] It is even said that some *karadji* masters can physically levitate while in trance, [11] and though there are no clear statements to the fact there are hints that they do this along dreaming tracks (see Sampler entry 47).

The dreaming tracks simultaneously run through the physical landscape and the inner – mental and spiritual – geography of the Aborigines. It is an interactive relationship between mind, body, soul and land that is quite unfamiliar to modern Westerners.

CHAPTER TWO

Roads of the Dead

There is a special class of old pathway or road in Europe called a "corpse road". In Britain it might also be known by a number of other names -bier road, burial road, coffin line, lyke or lych way (from Old English *liches*, corpse), or funeral road, to mention just some of them. The term is also found as far back as Saxon times as *deada waeg*, which may be the etymological roots of the Dutch term for corpse roads, *Doodwegen* ("deathroads").[1] The Dutch also have a variety of related terms (see Sampler entry 44), as do the Germans (see Sampler entry 29). A corpse road is usually synonymous with a church path or churchway – that is, a road specifically for going to and from a church – but that is not necessarily always the case (by and large, though, the terms are used interchangeably in this book). In Ireland a churchway can sometimes be referred to as a "Mass road" (Sampler entry 41), while in Germany or the Netherlands the term is usually *kirchweg* or *kirkweg*.

Corpse roads are primarily medieval features – though some are of a later time, dating from the Early Modern period – and consequently many have disappeared while the original purposes of those that survive as footpaths have been largely forgotten. Historians generally consider them to be minor features.

The basic, material facts concerning corpse roads are straightforward enough: they provided a functional means of allowing walking or packhorse funerals to transport corpses to cemeteries that had burial rights. In England in the tenth century, for instance, burial rights became an issue with the beginning of a great expansion of church building, which inevitably encroached on the territories of existing mother churches or minsters. There was a demand for autonomy from outlying settlements that minster officials felt could erode their authority, not to mention their revenue, so they decided to institute corpse ways that led from outlying locations to the mother church at the heart of the parish, the one that alone held the burial rights. For some parishioners this meant corpses had to be transported quite long distances, sometimes over difficult terrain.

Furniture of the Death Roads
Most of the funerals conducted along corpse roads were walking ones, with teams of bearers carrying the coffin or bier, which was a wooden stretcher supporting a stiff canvas bag into which the corpse was sewn.[2] Alternatively,

depending on the period, region, and the nature of the corpse road, mourners accompanied the corpse loaded on a packhorse or laid in a cart, which was also often referred to as the bier. For both practical and ritual reasons the coffin or bier would need resting at various points along the way so the bearers or draft ponies could rest, and hymns sung or prayers said over the dearly departed. Traditional stopping places included the steps of preaching crosses (see Sampler entry 13). In Cornwall, small, round-headed Celtic wayside

Fig. 1. A wayside Cornish cross. This one is on a churchway leading to St Levan from Ardensawah. (Arthur Langdon, Old Cornish Crosses, 1896)

crosses marked the footpaths of the Land's End district, which had few roads suitable for wheeled traffic until recent centuries (Figure 1). In particular, as W. Haslam remarked in 1847, the function of many of the crosses was to "guard and guide the way to the church". He went on: "In several parishes there are 'church paths', still kept up by the parish, along which crosses, or bases of crosses, yet remain, and generally it will be found that they point toward the church." [3]

Fig. 2. Coffin stone at a granite stile. (Walter Field, Stones of the Temple, 1876)

These also often became the places where walking funerals would rest the coffin and conduct hymn singing or prayers.

Resting places at least as common as crosses were often rough-hewn "coffin stones", a variety of examples of which are shown in the Sampler in Part Two (see entries 7 and 16). Sometimes, stones might be set at stiles for the same purpose (Figure 2).

When the funeral cortege reached the boundary of the churchyard it went through a special gate, for the boundary around a holy place is properly known as a *temenos,* a perimeter between the sacred and the mundane that is fraught with ritual significance. The gate was, of course, the lych-gate, the corpse-gate, and it would be the final stopping point prior to entering the church (Figure 3). The lych-gate would often be equipped with a roof to help

Fig. 3. A lych-gate. (Water Field, 1876)

shelter mourners from rain or shine if they arrived too early for the service (for travel along corpse roads did not allow for exact timing), and almost always with a special wooden or stone shelf for the coffin to be rested on. A medieval wooden plinth survives in the lych-gate of St Mary's church at Chiddingfold, Surrey (Plate 1), and a stone one centuries old is still to be found on the boundary of St Leven's churchyard in Cornwall (see Sampler entry 3). Most lych-gate coffin stones that are now to be found, though, take the simple form of a thin slab running longitudinally through the middle of the gate's opening.

It was popularly believed that if a walking funeral crossed someone's land then it would thereafter become a public right of way, and though this never seems to have been the case in law many landowners were not keen on allowing such funeral processions passage across their property. Consequently, corpse ways tended to followed established routes to the church, and these were typically the churchway paths used by worshippers from outlying farms and communities to attend church on Sundays and holy days.

Fields crossed by churchway paths often had names like "Churchway Field" to identify the special routes passing through them, and it is sometimes possible to plot the course of a churchway by old field names even after the path itself has disappeared

A Secret History

These basic facts about medieval corpse roads in Britain do not tell the whole story about them. They also possess a secret history involving the beliefs and practices of the rural

Plate 1. The ancient coffin plinth at the lych-gate of Chiddingfold church, Surrey.

people who used them, which tends to slip below the "radar" of standard, mainstream history. As the scholar Carlo Ginzburg has observed, historians are poor at studying "invisible mental structures" of this kind.[4] Corpse ways attracted spirit lore already long extant in isolated rural populations, for they ran not only through the physical countryside but also through the invisible country, the mental terrain, of pre-industrial countryfolk. Vestiges of this archaic spirit lore are revealed by a variety of "virtual" and physical features across Old Europe.

The virtual features were folk beliefs that had a geographical reality. An example existed in Nemen, Russia (in a region that was formerly eastern Prussia), where there was the tradition of a *Leichenflugbahn,* literally "corpse flightpath". There were two cemeteries in the town, one Lithuanian, the other German, and the spirits of those interred in them were believed to be able to travel between the two places. These ghosts were said to fly along on a direct course close to the ground, so a straight line connecting the two places was kept clear of fences, walls, and buildings so that they would not be obstructed. An apocryphal tale tells of a local man who wished to erect a shed between the two cemeteries, but obviously did not want to have it protrude directly onto the spirits' flightpath. As he had "second sight" enabling him to see spirits, he marked the passage of the flitting phantoms by placing a stick in the ground and erecting his shed just to one side of it (this theme of seers able to perceive spectres on spirit routes is a recurring one, as we shall learn). Unfortunately, the man's psychic abilities did not prevent him from being careless, for a corner of the roof projected a tiny amount onto the flightpath, resulting in the shed being flattened. He re-erected it "a hundred" times but with the same outcome, so it seems the fellow was a slow learner.[5]

The Germans had virtual paths they called *Geisterwege* that linked actual, physically real cemeteries. Although invisible, these spirit paths had a definite geography in local folklore, and people would be sure to avoid them at night. They also were straight; a German folklore reference work describes them thus:

> The paths, with no exception, always run in a straight line over
> mountains and valleys and through marshes ... In towns they pass
> the houses closely or go right through them. The paths end or
> originate at a cemetery. This idea may stem from the ancient custom
> of driving a corpse along a special dead man's road, therefore this
> way or road was believed to have the same characteristics as a
> cemetery, it is a place where spirits of deceased thrive.[6]

In Ireland and other Celtic lands there were straight fairy paths that while being invisible nevertheless had such perceived geographical reality in the minds of the country people that building practices were adopted to ensure their unobstructed passage (see Chapter Three). Fairies and the spirits of the dead held a curiously ambiguous relationship in the peasant mind: for instance, American folklorist Evans Wentz was told about paths of the dead in Brittany that he could not distinguish from the beliefs about fairy paths elsewhere. The specific Breton tradition related to the *Ankou,* the last man to die in a parish during the year. For the next twelve months he was King of the Dead, and he and his subjects "like a fairy king and fairies, have their own particular paths or roads over which they travel in great sacred processions".[7] The perceived nature of these Breton paths is unfortunately not described, though most if not all of these and other virtual spirit paths seem to have been conceived of as being straight.

The actual, physical corpse roads of Europe vary between being perfectly straight and not particularly straight at all. Straight ones include a curious Viking funeral path at Rosaring in Sweden, which runs in a straight line to a Viking and Bronze Age cemetery in Sweden,[8] a stone road in the Hartz Mountains in Germany (see Sampler entry 31), and the Dutch *Doodwegen,* which were officially checked on an annual basis to ensure their straightness and regular width and appear to be rather more exact versions of British corpse roads.

So, in Europe in former times, there seems to have been a "virtual blueprint" concerning spirit ways relating to physical cemeteries and physical, more pragmatic paths actually used for conveying corpses to burial. The precise relationship between these virtual and physical features has not been fully explored, but there is no doubt that the physical corpse roads came to be perceived as being spirit routes, taking on aspects of the "virtual blueprint". It may not be a tidy transposition for mainstream historians but it is nevertheless undeniable because it is documented. For a start, there is an abundance of generalized lore about how corpses were to be conveyed along corpse roads to avoid their spirits returning along them to haunt the living. It was a widespread custom, for example, that the feet of the corpse should be kept pointing away from the family home on its journey to the cemetery. Other minor ritualistic means of preventing the return of the dead person's shade included ensuring that the route the corpse took to burial would take it over bridges or stepping stones across streams (for spirits could not cross open, running water), stiles, and various other liminal ("betwixt and between") locations, all of which had reputations for preventing or hindering the free passage of spirits. In old Europe, crossroads were included as another such place (the corpses of suicides were buried at crossroads, for example, so that their spirits would be "bound" there, and for similar reasons gallows were often erected at them). In Ireland, the coffin or bier would be carried in a sunwise circle around "some place or object on the way, a cross, a church-site, a lone thorn tree or a crossroads".[9] It was at such locations along the corpse road that the coffin would be rested and the prayers said or hymns sung, as mentioned earlier. Finally, it was generally considered "unlucky" to take a corpse to burial by a route other than the customary corpse way. What this surely meant was that if the body was not taken by this route, the ghost of the departed might return to haunt its neighbours and relatives, or would wander the land as a lost soul – or even as an animated corpse, for the belief in revenants was widespread in medieval Europe.[10]

All these customary precautions against haunting by a dead person's ghost obviously suggest that people using the corpse roads assumed that they could be a passage for the spirits of the dead, but in any case there is more specific evidence. A documented contemporary tradition relating to a corpse road at Aalst, Belgium, informs that mourners had to intone: "Spirit, proceed ahead, I'll follow you". This suggests that the spirit connection was alive and well when the roads were being used, and is not some falsified folk memory added later. This is further indicated by the fact that one Dutch term for a corpse road was *Spokenweg*, ghost road (see Sampler entry 44). Furthermore, ghostly happenings were thought to occur on death roads in the Netherlands, which was a good reason to avoid these routes at night.[11]

German lore similarly maintained that corpse roads took on the "magical characteristics of the dead" and should not be obstructed – an interesting similarity to the folklore concerning fairy paths (see Chapter Three and Sampler entries in the Irish section). British corpse ways were also definitely associated with spirits. This is not only shown in the widespread folk belief that old paths leading to and from cemeteries needed to be swept so as to dislodge spirits haunting them, or "spirits traps" (webs of thread) placed on them to snare flitting phantoms, but also in the works of Shakespeare. The Bard specifically confirms the believed association between spirits and corpse roads in his *A Midsummer Night's Dream*, where he has that old land spirit, Puck, pronounce in his penultimate speech:

> *Now it is the time of night,*
> *That the graves all gaping wide,*

Every one lets forth his sprite,
In the church-way paths to glide.

There it is, the secret history of corpse roads revealed by the most noble of pens.

Church and Folk Conflict

It is not surprising that pathways used for such a dread activity as transporting dead bodies should attract spirit lore: as historian Nancy Caciola has remarked, "spirits seeking bodies haunted the late medieval landscape".[12] In the medieval and early modern periods there was a schism between the Church and the rural populations of Europe with regard to supernatural ideas. The populace was held in thrall by older motifs to do with the "unruly dead" and the old gods disguised as Christian saints, and not theological constructs. But Caciola also points out: "Even as these two systems of thought competed with one another . . . they overlapped."

A key aspect of this schism was that the Church taught that the spirit left the body at death and went immediately to another, non-physical plane (heaven, hell, or purgatory), while rural communities believed that the dead could return and haunt the locality. Ordinary countryfolk felt they shared the land with spirits, as was the case with virtually every other ancient society on Earth. The Church taught an abstract cosmology while country populations stubbornly inhabited a literal one. "In all tales we find the survival of the medieval connection between ghosts and locality, " historian Bruce Gordon has emphasized.[13] Countryfolk worried about "ghostes and spirites walking by nyght" no matter what their priests proclaimed.

Corpse Roads and Necromancy

The spirit connection with the physical corpse way has more subtle confirmation. It is a fair surmise that there was a link between corpse ways and the strange practice known in Britain as the "church porch watch" or "sitting-up".[14] In this practice, a village seer – known variously as a ghost-seer, church-watcher, a wise-woman (or man), or simply as a witch, wizard or fortune-teller – would hold a vigil between 11 p.m. and 1 a.m. at the church door, lych-gate (where the corpse road entered), in the graveyard, or on a nearby lane (this presumably had to be a corpse road to make the procedure effective), in order to look for the wraiths of those who would die in the following twelve-month period. Typically, this took place on St Mark's Eve (24 April), Hallowe'en, or the eves of New Year, Midsummer, or Christmas. The wraiths, sometimes called "doubles", of the doomed living members of the community would usually appear to the inner eye of the seer as a procession coming in from beyond the churchyard and passing into the church door, and then returning back out into the night. Some churchyards where it is known seers performed their watch include those at Bridlington, Driffield, Easington, Flamborough, Kelnsey and Patrington in East Yorkshire, Wakefield in West Yorkshire, Northorpe and Winterton in Lincolnshire, Stalham in Norfolk, Walesby in Nottinghamshire, and Buckland in Dorset (see Sampler entry 12). There were of course a great many more throughout Britain. The names of some of the seers have also come down to us: a woman called Milkey Lawrence was active at Flamborough, Ben Barr, known locally as a prophet, conducted the watch at a church in Northamptonshire, Katherine Foxegale was a ghost-seer at Walesby and was hauled before a Church court in 1608, "Old Peggy Richard" did the business at Northorpe, and Margaret Dove ("Old Peg Doo") used to conduct her watch in the north porch of the Priory church at Bridlington.

In England, the phenomena supposedly witnessed by the seers was primarily visual in nature. Typical visions consisted of processions of doomed souls, or coffins containing those who were to die (in some places the spectral coffins were said to be transported by shadowy and often headless figures), but there were numerous variations on these themes. In some cases, especially in Wales, watchers were more likely to hear a disembodied voice tell the names of those who were soon to die. One apocryphal story tells of a church-watcher who saw a spectral form that was so hazy he had to lean forward to try to identify it. As he did so he heard a disembodied whisper break the still night air: "'Tis yourself!".

It is difficult to determine whether the true ghost-seers went into trance to have their visions, but there are hints that this was the case in the fact that fasting was a common preparation for watchers, and in the Faroe Islands only those who had "second sight" (natural visionary ability) were allowed to church watch.

It is a reasonable guess that the concept of spectral processions of people or coffins coming into the churchyard would have been related to the corpse ways or church paths leading there. This is supported by the fact that some seers witnessed spectral funerals rather than the wraiths of living people, and is further hinted at in a record relating to an old woman at Fryup, Yorkshire, who was well-known locally for keeping the "Mark's e'en watch" and lived alongside a corpse road known as the "Old Hell Way" (see Sampler entry 22).

The antiquity of ghost-seership is probably considerable, but it only began to be documented in a Christian context in Britain from the seventeenth century. It was sporadically mentioned over the following two centuries, during which period the old custom became diluted into superstition by people daring one another to conduct a watch or into general divination by those seeking future knowledge of secular matters such as trade or marriage. By the beginning of the twentieth century it appears to have all but ceased due to changing social conditions.

The church porch watch custom in Britain may have been a less-structured variant of a Dutch tradition concerning a class of diviners called *voorlopers* or *veurkieken*, "precursors", who were specifically associated with the Dutch death roads, the *Doodwegen*.[15] They were seers able to tell who was soon to die in the community because they had the ability to see spectral funeral processions pass along the death road they visited or lived alongside. Folkorist W Y Evans Wentz recorded a similar tradition near Carnac in Brittany.[16]

An echo of corpse road necromancy is probably preserved in the folklore theme of the "phantom funeral", known in Wales as the *toeli*. The classic account of this type relates to a reported event in Cardiganshire, Wales, in 1816. It had been an exceptionally wet harvest, and so when a fine evening came along farmers took the opportunity to stay out late binding the corn into sheaves, as plenty of light was being cast by the harvest moon. A farmer and his wife were busy at work in a field of their small farm when they heard the hum of voices in the distance. It was coming from a crowd walking along the "parish road" that passed unfenced through the field they were in – it was a churchway. As the crowd drew close to them the farming couple saw that it was accompanying a coffin on a bier. "The binders heard the tramp of feet and the sound of voices, but not a syllable could they comprehend of what was said, not a face could they recognize," wrote schoolmaster William Jenkyn Thomas, who collected the account directly from the farmer and his wife. "They kept their eyes on the procession till it went out of sight on the way leading towards the parish church."[17] The same funeral party was encountered by another local person, a tailor, further along toward the church where the road had become hedged. He had to get out of the procession's way, as it filled the whole road. The witnesses thought little more of the event until three weeks later when a real funeral procession "came down that way from the upper end of the parish".[18] (An example of a *toeli* is to be found in Sampler entry 28.) This type of sighting bears a close similarity to the "fairy funeral" – see Chapter Three.

The Dutch precursors, the Breton funeral seers, and the British churchyard watchers would seem to fall into the same general class of divination as those who perceived the spirits of the dead in trance by "sitting out" *(utiseta)* in cemeteries or on burial mounds in old Norse tradition, or

Plate 2. According to researcher Phil Quinn (The Ley Hunter, no. 128, 1997) this crossroads on Coldchange Hill, Gloucestershire, was a resting place on a corpse road between Hillesley and Hawkesbury. The spot was said to be haunted by spectral monks. The course of the corpse road continues straight on now as a footpath through a gate and past the large tree.

by sitting entranced at certain times between St Lucy's Day (13 December) and Christmas – a seership custom known in Hungary as "St Lucy's Stool".

Another facet of this same general class of seership was almost certainly that described in Icelandic folklore, which concerned a medieval practice at crossroads "where four roads run, each in a straight unbroken line, to four churches", or from where four churches were visible. The seer would go to such a crossroads on New Year's Eve, or St John's Day and cover himself with the hide of a bull or a walrus, and fix his attention on the shiny blade of an axe while laying as still as a corpse throughout the night. He would recite various spells to summon the spirits of the dead from the church cemeteries and they would glide up the roads to the crossroads where the seer could divine information from them.[19] Crossroads divination was also conducted in former times in Britain and other parts of Europe, and it has already been noted that they were one type of location favoured as stopping points on corpse roads (Plate 2).[20]

There was yet another form of associated necromantic divination. Entry 1 in the Sampler in Part Two gives an account of a Cornish folktale in which the ghost of a woman's dead husband carries her over the tree-tops and deposits her on a church stile where she is able to interrogate passing ghosts, and then carries her back, during which journey she loses a shoe in some tree branches:

this would appear to be a folk-gloss of a corpse road as being a passage of spirits, and also illumines an obscure piece of folklore that relates to a practice known as "stile divination", particularly common in Wales where it was said that stiles were "favourite perches for ghosts".[21] The problem hitherto has been that stile divination was mentioned in the folk record without its context being known.

Gone with the Wind

In its account of the spectral husband carrying the widow to the church stile, the Cornish folktale also provides a curious echo of a strange piece of fairylore, once particularly common in Wales. This stated that living human beings (or their spirits) could be transported through the air by fairies (see Sampler entry 26). It was said that the person was always given the option of flying "above wind, mid wind, or below wind".[22] The last mode often led to collisions with trees and other objects – much as seems to have happened to the Cornish widow. The Cornish story highlights the ambivalence that existed in the folk mind between fairies and the dead, and is essentially the same image as that involving the spirit path between the two cemeteries at Nemen described earlier, which in turn is remarkably similar to ideas about *Geisterwege* and other "virtual" spirit roads.

Origins

Once it is understood that corpse roads had necromantic associations, their spirit-road nature becomes clear, and it is possible to recognize references to the fact in fragments of old lore from all over Europe. Behind all these fragments the outlines of a coherent body of spirit lore can be faintly discerned, a corpus of spirit beliefs that persisted in the "virtual" spirit paths traversing the folk mindscapes of old Europe and also became attached to the actual, physical corpse roads – even if in a disjointed manner. Though corpse roads are in themselves Medieval or Early Modern features, the spirit lore that became attached to them probably had its roots in ancient shamanic traditions, for contact with the ancestral spirits and spirit flight are quintessential shamanic themes. Throughout Medieval and Early Modern Europe, from Hungary and Italy in the southeast to Ireland and Scandinavia in the northwest, and almost everywhere in between, there were for untold generations various traditions concerning trance practitioners. These took the form of village specialists who could enter an ecstatic mode of consciousness – the hallmark of shamanism – in order to conduct divination, to protect the fertility of the fields, livestock and vineyards by means of "night battles" against hostile sorcerers, or to obtain magical power. These specialists from different countries and periods of history often shared similar characteristics, and some scholars claim that they belonged to a common origin of great antiquity: an agrarian shamanism that stretched from Asia to Western Europe.[23] Beliefs in vampires and werewolves are also considered to have arisen out of this.[24]

CHAPTER THREE

Fairies and their Paths

The spirits we refer to as fairies have haunted the countryside in many lands throughout the world. The best-known tradition in the West is that belonging to the Celtic countries on Europe's western fringe. Here, belief in fairies was strong until a few generations ago, and still lingers among the older population. In the Celtic tradition, fairies were entities who were barred from paradise. They inhabited a middle kingdom between the human world and the Otherworld of the dead – though, as we shall see, that was frequently a somewhat blurred distinction. They lived in and moved around the land, but were invisible to the human inhabitants most of the time. Contact between the human and fairy races was most often indirect: fairies would be heard and not seen, their effects felt (such as good/bad luck, illness), and notice taken of changes they made to house, farmyard or field. The places that they were believed to inhabit or haunt were treated with fear and respect because it was known that interference with them could cause misfortune. Certain protocols had to be followed in order for humans to keep on good terms with the fairies, who at the best of times could be mischievous and were nearly always a little touchy. All in all, sharing the land with the fairies was a delicate and, at times, dangerous business.

The Fairy Races

The fairies of old folklore were not the sweet, butterfly-winged creatures of the Victorian fairylore revival. "The metamorphosis from savage nature spirits to the twee sprites of Victorian fancy was the artistic counterpart of the taming of the wild, natural world by industry and human rationality," David Sivier perceptively observes.[1] Medieval and Early Modern fairies flew by means of casting spells, or by riding on twigs, straws, stems of ragwort, butterflies or moths, and so had no need of gossamer wings.

There was a multitude of types making up the fairy races, and though most were essentially anthropomorphic, there were also fairy animals such as black dogs (which could also occasionally be other colours) and even a few shapeless horrors. The humanoid kind appear in the folkloric record variously as tall men known as the "Gentry" in Ireland, as beautiful human-like maidens or wizened old crones, as dwarf-like creatures, and even smaller beings from a few to several inches in height, and as elemental sprites. Fairies could be exquisitely-formed creatures or misshapen, grotesque beings. In European traditions fairies came to have many names covering the whole spectrum of types: sprites, piskies and pixies, sylphs, undines and dryads, the *sidh* of Ireland, the usually kind *glaistigs* of the Scottish Highlands, the Welsh *Tylwyth Teg*, the wailing banshees of Ireland (see Sampler entry 34), and a host of other entities. In Cornwall there were underground spirits such as spriggans and knockers that the tin miners had to keep on the right side of. Certain fairy entities were distinctly sinister, such as water kelpies that sought to devour humans, the redcaps of the Scottish border (their headgear coloured by the blood of travellers they had killed), the ugly yarthkins of the Lincolnshire fens, and the child-eating Black Annis of the English Midlands.

Strange lights were almost always interpreted as fairies, or lanterns held in their small and invisible hands.[2] For instance, in County Mayo, Ireland, the earthwork of Crillaun was said to blaze with small, winking white lights from time to time, and these were naturally assumed to be fairies.[3] By the same token, lights seen flickering on marshland were known as Will-o'-the-Wisp, traditionally interpreted as being a mischievous land spirit ready to lead travellers astray – or "pixy-lead" them, as was said in Devon.[4] In Wales, mysterious lights were called "corpse candles" *(canwyll corfe)* and were thought to forewarn of a death (Sampler entry 28).

There was also a specific class of fairy creature that the folklorist Katharine Briggs referred to as "hobmen"; these were mainly solitary beings and were given such names as hob, hobgoblin, brownie, boggart, elf, Robin Goodfellow, and, of course, Puck. A hobman could be a wild, country spirit, or a house fairy "that doth haunt hearth and dairy".[5]

One term for a house fairy in England was the charming lob-lie-by-the-fire. In Wales the being was known as a *bwbach,* and described as being brown and often hairy. An old Cornish account of a brownie offers a similar description: " . . . a little old man, no more than three feet [90 cm] high, covered with only a few rags, and his long hair hung over his shoulders like a bunch of rushes . . . His face was broader than it was long . . . He had nothing of a chin or neck to speak of, but shoulders broad enow for a man twice his height. His naked arms and legs were out of all proportion, and too long for his squat body; and his splayed feet were more like a quilkan's (frog's) than a man's".[6] In Scotland, by contrast, the brownie was thought of as being a tall man. The relationship between farmer or householder and the domestic fairy had to be a carefully controlled one – the spirit would do certain chores provided it was treated well, but was capable of causing harm if it felt it was not being respected.

Country hobmen or land spirits haunted wild, uncultivated locations. In his *The Faithful Shepherdess,* the playwright John Fletcher manages to mention several land spirits and make an allusion to fairy lights as well:

> *No Goblin, Wood-god, Fairy, Fife or Fiend,*
> *Satyr or other power that haunts the Groves,*
> *Shall hurt my body, or by vain illusion*
> *Draw me to wander after idle fires.*

Puck is known in various lands and regions by cognate names such as the Irish animal spirit – often taking the form of a black dog – known as the *Pooka,*[7] the Welsh *Pwca* and *Bwca,* and the French *Pouque.* It is of course also the root of the term "pixies" or, in Cornwall, "piskies". Puck is a generalized personification of all the land spirits; he is an aspect of Robin Goodfellow, he is hob, he is Will-o'-the-Wisp. He is a prankster who "oft out of a Bush doth bolt, Of purpose to deceive us" as Drayton warns in his *Nimphidia.*

An intriguing factor concerning fairies is that they tended to share virtually identical characteristics with witches' familiars (the spirits who aided and abetted their supernatural activities).[8] "There had been a clear connection between fairy-lore and at least some forms of witchcraft from very early times," Katherine Briggs has acknowledged.[9] A Cornish folktale, for example, combines witch-lore and fairy-lore in its account of how the infamous Cornish witch, Madge Figgy, would fly out from the sea cliffs at night on a stem of ragwort.

Puritans considered fairies to be devils, and fairies, witches' familiars, and demons merged and mixed in a late Medieval and Early Modern conceptual merry-go-round.

Fairy Etiquette
In spite of the variety of types, fairies displayed fairly common traits. They had superhuman powers such as flight, invisibility, and shape-shifting. As the seventeenth-century Scottish minister and collector of fairylore, Robert Kirk, put it: "Their bodies of congealed air are sometimes carried aloft, other whiles grovel in different shapes." All of them could be tricksters, ready to play pranks on mortals, while many were able and willing to punish human beings who annoyed them by inflicting quite serious ailments or causing cattle and domestic animals to become sick or die. They could also *take* – that is, abduct – mortals, whisking them off to fairyland never to be seen again, or lead them astray out into the night. So how people behaved toward them was considered to be a crucial issue.

In Celtic tradition, a key rule of fairy etiquette was to be indirect in talking about such spirit beings, and then to use a complimentary term. So fairies would typically be referred to as the "Good People" or "Gentle Folk" in Ireland. In Wales, the *Tylwyth Teg* means "the fair family", and other euphemistic terms included *Bendith y Mamau*, "the mother's blessing", and even the bizarre *Plant Rhys Dwfyn*, "the children of Rhys and the Deep". If fairies happened to be directly encountered one had to be courteous towards them, and above all to politely decline eating or drinking fairy food, otherwise enchantment – the Rip Van Winkle effect – was bound to ensue.

Fairies abhorred untidy manners and it was considered advisable to leave the house neat at night, with the hearth swept and the fire made up in case *they* visited nocturnally. It was also a good idea to leave a piece of cake or other morsel overnight to keep the fairies happy, and a suit of clothes should be left to repay a helpful domestic fairy such as a brownie. Fairies particularly liked milk, which could be left in a saucer by the hearth or poured over the ground outside the house; fairies were known to draw blood from hapless hosts who had not otherwise provided for them. Because fairies disliked human beings who interfered with their orderly ways, humans were wise not to obstruct their paths and to warn fairy folk before throwing out dirty water or the night's ashes.

If relations between a human household and fairies deteriorated despite all the appropriate diplomacy, there were various actions usually inimical to fairies that could be tried. These included uttering special prayers or sayings, using iron, wielding a black-handled knife, hazel stick or fire-ember, or sprinkling a fairy or its haunt with holy water. Fairies could also be banished by the crowing of a cock (which had a similar effect on witches and vampires) and, like most spirits, they could not cross running water.

Fairy Places
In Ireland, locales haunted or frequented by fairies were referred to by such euphemisms as "gentle" or "airy" (eerie) places. Major among them were circular earthworks known variously as "fairy forts", *raths*, or lisses *(lios)* among other appellations. Over two thousand of these ring-forts are to be found scattered across the Irish landscape. They usually take the form of circular areas defined by a bank and ditch, often on a knoll or rise in the ground, and now often fringed by thorn bushes or surmounted by a copse. They originated in the Iron Age as fortified dwelling sites, but many of the visible enclosures today date from between A.D.500–1200, and a few were in

Plate 3. Lios Ard fairy fort, Kiltimagh, Co. Mayo, Ireland.

use until the seventeenth century. Certain ring-forts have underground stone-built chambers or passages thought by archaeologists to have been used for dwelling or storage. To generations of country people these forts – or "forths" as they are often pronounced – were seen as one of the most important types of place where the fairies dwelt, living underground, and from which they emerged at night. A fine and famous example of such a site is Lios Ard ("High Fort"), near Kiltimagh in County Mayo (Plate 3). A fellow called Martin Brennan told the Irish historian and folklorist, Dermot Mac Manus, that one summer evening he was working in a field below Lios Ard called "Outer Background" when he noticed a score or more human-sized fairy folk on the fort's slopes. The women had their heads covered by shawls while some of the men wore conical hats. Their coats were red or brown in colour. These strange people were good-looking but had startlingly noticeable "penetrating, staring eyes".[10]

There is also an old spreading oak tree at the foot of Lios Ard around which the fairies are said to dance at certain times of the year, and where the blind folk poet, Anthony Raftery, is said to have been offered the gift of poetry and music by the fairies. This highlights another key kind of fairy site in Ireland: certain trees or bushes. The Irish tradition of sacred trees, *bile,* goes back into dim prehistory: archaeologists found that the Iron-Age hilltop site of Navan Fort in Armagh, Northern Ireland, for instance, had once sported a ritual post 39 ft (12 m) tall that had been fashioned from a two-hundred-year-old oak tree.[11] The association of fairies – and sometimes spirits of the dead – with certain thorn bushes is probably an ancient variation on the sacred tree theme. Being such a common tree, most thorns were not considered to have fairy associations, so what made one stand out? Typically, fairy thorns are those that are "conspicuously alone" (see Sampler entry 37), whether in the middle of a field or in a hedgerow, or that grow near wells or in fairy forts. Otherwise, it was usually because fairies or shadowy figures had been seen near a bush, or because someone had suffered bad fortune after damaging one. (It is worth remarking here that the old beliefs underwent a resurgence when catastrophe

Plate 4. The distinctive and solitary fairy hill of Glastonbury Tor silhouetted on the Somerset skyline.

struck the luxury car-maker John DeLorean because it was widely rumoured that a fairy bush had been uprooted during the building of his Belfast factory.) Various other beliefs concerning fairy trees include that they scream or bleed if cut, their wood will not burn, treasure is buried beneath their roots, and many others. Milk was sometimes poured around the roots of identified fairy trees for the Good People.

A third important category of fairy place in Celtic tradition involves the "fairy mountain": fairies were thought to dwell inside certain hills and mountains. The singular conical peak of Glastonbury Tor in England (Plate 4) was considered a major fairy site: the striking, solitary hill was said to have harboured the fairy king himself, Gwynn ap Nudd. At least it did until St Collen banished him and his glittering entourage by throwing holy water over them. A prevailing folkloric theme associated with fairy hills (and prehistoric burial mounds) concerned human beings who happened across the fairy entrances to them and discovered a glittering fairyland within. The mortals concerned would never be seen or heard of again, as exemplified in the folktale of the Pied Piper of Hamelin, or else they would become enchanted, and return only decades or centuries later. A parallel strand of lore (particularly in northern lands such as Iceland) maintained that the spirits of the dead also lived within hills. In fact, even as far afield as North America some Indian societies believed spirits inhabited the interior of hills and cliff-faces.

Apart from fairy forts (in Ireland), trees, and hills, other natural locations favoured by the fairies included springs and certain pools and lakes (Sampler entries 34 and 38), caves (Sampler entry 39), and wild spots such as rock outcrops and small valleys. Some of these places can still be identified by their names. To take a few examples in England, there is Goblin Combe in the Bristol area, and also Goblin Ledge on the Severn Beach. A large natural rock in Dorset is called the Puckstone.[12] On and around Dartmoor, there is Pixies Parlour, a tumble of boulders near the Fingle Gorge, a huge boulder called the Puggie Stone near Chagford, and the Pixies House, a granite grotto with a narrow cleft as an opening on Sheepstor where offerings of pins or pieces of rags used to be left for the pixies.[13] The fading laughter of Puck echoes in all these place-names, as it does in many others around the country.

Apart from these types of selected natural places, fairies also became associated with some of the prehistoric earthen and stone monuments to be found in Ireland, Britain and Continental Europe. It was believed that prehistoric burial mounds, barrows, were inhabited by fairies, so there is in Wales, for example, a barrow known as Bryn-yr-Ellyllon, "Hill of Elves", or in Dorset there was a Puck's Barrow near Winfrith Newburgh. In Norse lore elves typically lived in ancient burial mounds. A classic piece of English folklore originating in the twelfth century attaches itself to the large Neolithic mound of Willy Howe in Yorkshire. It tells of a horseman passing by it on his way home one night. On hearing singing coming from within the barrow he stopped to investigate and discovered an entrance. Peering in, he saw men and women in the glowing interior enjoying a feast. A goblet of wine was offered to the traveller, but he realized that he was encountering fairies and so he snatched it, poured away its contents, and rode off with it at such speed that the outraged fairies could not catch him.

Between Aldershot and Farnborough in Hampshire, there is a traffic island with the curious – and ancient – name of Cockadobby Hill. It has been analysed as meaning "major hobgoblin": "cocker", as in the Cockney "My old cocker", means boss, and "dobby" is a term for goblin.[14] The traffic island stands on the site of a Romano-British or later barrow, but various inconclusive excavations have suggested that this surmounted a prehistoric mound. In former times, the mound had four tracks leading to it, and these eventually became the motor roads that now meet at this point. In the late nineteenth century, a soldier at a nearby army camp was standing on guard duty facing toward Cockadobby Hill when something struck his sentry box. Gripping his rifle, he peered into the night to see a dark, flitting figure taking huge leaps. Perhaps it was a hobgoblin still playing its pranks . . .

The idea of "hollow" hills inhabited by fairies extended to prehistoric burial mounds, and there are legends of spirits coming out of such mounds to advise the living, or of shepherds falling asleep on the mounds and having inspirational dreams. These legends doubtless stem from the necromantic tradition of "sitting out", mentioned in the previous chapter.

Stone sites were also associated with fairies. For instance, it was believed that the prehistoric cup markings made on (usually horizontal) rock surfaces in many parts of Atlantic Europe were for libations to the elves, perhaps explaining why sun-wheel carvings common in Scandinavian rock-art were sometimes referred to as the "glory of the elves". In Normandy and the Channel Islands megalithic sites are sometimes referred to as *Pouquelaie*, and other names hinting at fairy connections survive in England. One of the stones in the Hordron Edge stone circle in Derbyshire, as one example, has been known as the "fairy stone" for unknown generations. It is only one of several "fairy stones" in Britain.

Fairy Paths

As mentioned earlier, fairies could fly on winged insects or plant stalks, or they could simply fly through the air of their own volition. They also trooped along special paths that belonged to them. Robert Kirk stated that fairies could "swim in the air near the earth".[15] A specific instance was described by an eighteenth-century Welsh witness:

> Edmund Daniel of the Arail, an Honest Man, and a constant
> speaker of the truth, and of much observation, told me, that he
> often saw them [the fairies] after Sun-set, crossing the Keven
> Bach, from the Valley of the Church, towards Havodavel . . .
> leaping and frisking in the Air, making a path in the Air . . . [16]

Terrestrial fairy paths – what Kirk called their "secret paths" – connected fairy places generally, and, in Ireland, the fairy forts in particular. Typically, fairy thorns were markers or stations along these invisible routes. The paths were usually used by "trooping fairies", often on their way to battles with other groups of fairies, but other times just by fairies generally to go about their fairy business, about which mortals need not enquire.

But what exact form were fairy paths understood to take? People very often fail to describe roads or routes, omitting to mention whether they were winding or straight, or exactly where their courses ran, concentrating solely on where they start and finish. This is usually the case with folklore sources concerning fairy paths. My father, who was a rural Irishman, always assumed fairy paths were straight, and collectors of fairy-lore, such as Dermot Mac Manus, made a similar assumption (see below). Indeed, virtually all the (admittedly sparse) evidence suggests that fairy tracks were straight. But controversy over the subject has arisen and one case in the literature had been cited to indicate that fairy paths were, in fact, crooked. It is mentioned in the famous book *The Fairy Faith in Celtic Countries* by the American folklorist, W Y Evans Wentz, who in the early years of the twentieth century visited all the Celtic lands and collected fairy lore verbatim from people who were elderly at that time. The case in contention concerned an account Evans Wentz was given to the effect that fairies from Rath Ringlestown in Ireland would form a procession, march forth across the land, and "pass round certain bushes which have not been disturbed for ages".[17] But did this actually describe a crooked route? It could have been the opposite, that the fairies were following a direct course marked by fairy bushes that they had to circumvent in order to proceed along it. This is clearly indicated by the folklorist Patrick Kennedy writing in 1870:

> It is known that the hill-folk [the fairies], in their nightly
> excursions, and in visits of one tribe to another, go in a straight
> line, gliding as it were within a short distance of the ground;
> and if they meet any strange obstacles in their track, they bend
> their course above them or at one side, but always with much
> displeasure.[18]

It would seem that fairy paths, like the invisible or "virtual" spirit routes mentioned in the previous chapter, were perceived to be straight, or at least straight for sections, before changing direction. Fairy paths seem to belong to a widespread and deep stratum of spirit lore, parts of which became attached to corpse roads.

The routes of fairy paths – also known as "passes", "passages", "avenues", "runs" – were said to coincide with lengths of old roads and lanes on those occasions where their respective courses agreed. Jimmy Armstrong, an informant of Clare folklorist Eddie Lenihan, explained that one reason people today do not see the strange things at night that folk long ago witnessed was because modern people "are goin' everywhere in cars these days and they have no time to see anything".[19] He continued: "But the real reason, I think, is the paths; no one is usin' the paths an' short-cuts through the land now compared to the gangs o' people that were usin' 'em years ago. There wasn't hardly a field where people didn't use to travel, day an' night . . ." Among the several eerie accounts Jimmy related to Lenihan was an encounter he had had in the 1930s with the mysterious figure of a man dressed in jet black. Jimmy was cycling along an unsurfaced country lane near a fairy fort at Ballyroughan, south-east of Sixmilebridge, in County Clare, in the early hours of the morning. The strange figure appeared from among thick whitethorn bushes, crossed over the road only a few feet in front of Jimmy's bicycle, walked down into a hollow in the road that contained a puddle of water, without making any sound nor taking any notice of Jimmy, and disappeared into the darkness. Later, Jimmy Armstrong learned that the priest from Sixmilebridge had also seen this curious dark figure on that road when returning from making parish calls late at night. In reply to Jimmy's enquiry as to who or what the "black man" was, the priest replied that he came "from the other world". Jimmy also learned that on the same road his grandfather used to have occasional early morning encounters with a black dog that padded along for a few hundred yards before vanishing at a small stream trickling across the road from a little spring. The folklore of Ireland and the British Isles tells that old roads and tracks were typically the haunts of spectral black dogs (see below).

Building Lore

Traditional building practice in Ireland was intimately related to fairy paths, for it was considered dangerous for a building to obstruct or impinge on one. The Irish writer and folklorist Lady Gregory found locals in Clare and Galway using the phrase "in the way" when talking about houses that had unlucky reputations. It became clear to her that the phrase referred to the obstruction of fairy paths.[20] Other terms often used for houses thought to block fairy paths was to say that they were "in a contrary place" or "in a path".

Dermot Mac Manus recorded several such instances personally known to him in western Ireland. One case he cited involved a fellow called Michael O'Hagan whose children were being taken ill and dying for no reason that the doctor could identify. O'Hagan sought advice from the local wise-woman. She came to his house, and immediately saw that an extension the man had built to the dwelling "obtruded into a straight line between two neighbouring fairy forts".[21] The extension was demolished and it was said that the man's remaining child grew up healthy. In another case, Mac Manus describes the problems that beset Paddy Baine's house near the Ox Mountains. The Baine household was plagued with poltergeist-like disturbances and Paddy had to seek advice from the famed wise-woman, Mairead ni Heine. She inspected the building and told Paddy that a corner of the house was interrupting a fairy path. He brought in a stonemason and had the corner flattened off, after which the disturbances ceased. (There are numerous houses in the western counties of Ireland with their corners modified, supposedly in order to correct problems resulting from encroachments onto fairy paths.) Even when care was taken problems could arise, it seems: Mickey Langan had identified a spot for his dwelling not far from the Baine's place and he carefully "looked at a few fairy forts", Mac Manus recounts. "He was not in a direct line between any two of them , and therefore his new home would in no way hinder the progress of the fairy hosts as they swept back and forth on their nightly expeditions".[22] But when he started digging the foundations, Mairead ni Heine cautioned him not to continue.

Lore regarding doors and fairy paths was universal in Ireland, and, it seems, throughout Europe. "When the house happens to have been built on a fairy track, the doors on the front and back, or the windows if they are in the line of the track, cannot be kept closed at night, for the fairies must [be allowed to] march through, " Evans Wentz was told by Irish informants.[23] Similarly, Moll Anthony, a wise-woman in County Laiose, informed a family suffering disturbances that "the cause o' your troubles are the big dures [doors] – the house is built on a fairy pass".[24] "Build up them dures, an' break out the other one, " she went on to advise. In other words, fill in the two side doors (which were opposite each other) and open up a new one at the end of the house. Other examples of door lore will be found in the Ireland section of the Sampler.

There were traditional ways of finding out if a planned building would obstruct a fairy path other than by consulting wise women. One was to warn the fairies of an intention to build at a spot. This was accomplished by placing four stones at what would be the corners of the intended building. A smaller stone was then placed on top of every one of these and left overnight; if they were in place in the morning then work could proceed, but if any had been knocked down then work had to be abandoned. A variant on this procedure was to insert sticks in the ground at each of the intended corners of the proposed house or barn, and if they were found knocked down the next morning then it was a sign that the fairies objected. Another fairy-friendly building practice was to select a site by standing in the designated field and throwing a hat into the air and building at the point where it had dropped out of the wind. Apart from identifying a location the fairies approved of, this had the happy side-effect of identifying a sheltered place.

General building lore in Ireland included the rule to avoid using white quartz in stonework when building anything, be it a field wall or a house, because quartz is a fairy stone. (Intriguingly, the Neolithic monuments in Ireland and elsewhere, made great use of quartz, and seemingly in a ritualistic way.) Another general – and rather curious – piece of lore warned not to extend a house in a westerly direction unless into space already artificially enclosed, such as a garden or yard. "To extend a house into a field or any open ground or across a path lying to the west is fatal," Mac Manus observed.[25]

Fairies and the Dead

It has been noted a number of times already in this book that fairies share an ambiguous relationship with spirits of the dead. "Ever since the first traceable beginnings of fairy beliefs the dead have been curiously entangled with fairies in popular tradition," Katherine Briggs noted.[26] The Hungarian folk scholar, Eva Pocs, similarly observes that there is a characteristic fairy mythology connected with the dead, and that in some examples of folklore "the fairies and the dead . . . are practically the same creatures".[27] Lady Gregory noted that there was a belief in the west of Ireland that the dead and fairies were different kinds of spirit, but that they mingled with one another, so that when the fairies pass by in a blast of wind we should say some words of blessing "for there may be among them some of our own dead". Evans Wentz was informed in Armagh that fairies were the spirits of dead friends, while in Brittany he was told that the dead were believed to continue inhabiting the same landscape as the living.[28] The American folklorist noted "how much the same are the powers and nature of the dead and spirits in Brittany, and the power and nature of the fairy races in Celtic Britain and Ireland".[29]

One way that this ambiguity between fairies and the dead is shown in Celtic tradition is in the relationship between fairies and funerals. Robert Kirk recorded that Scottish Highland people gifted with "second sight" can see fairies assisting humans in the carrying of the coffin to the grave. And Celtic fairy tradition tells of the fairy funeral, exemplified in a Cornish folktale, that tells of a man returning home one evening from St Ives who saw a light in Lelant church, in the sandhills near to the entrance of the creek at Hayle. He approached the church and peered in through a window. Amid the glow inside he saw a fairy funeral taking place. This motif is quite probably a reflex of the phantom funeral, the *toeli* of the Welsh described in Chapter Two. In Wales it was said that the *Tylwyth Teg,* in the form of small lights, "never fail going the way that the Corps will go to be buried".[30] All this presupposes a fairy link with corpse roads and churchways, a factor hinted at in an Irish tradition of lowering the funeral cross should the cortege pass a fairy thorn, or the already mentioned practice of encircling a thorn *en route* to the cemetery. The nineteenth-century Irish folklore collector, Thomas Keightley, recorded an account that probably related to this link: an informant told of seeing a procession of fairies travelling "across the High Field, in the direction o' the ould church".[31] An account given to Dermot Mac Manus by a Mrs C Woods concerning an experience she had on Haytor, Dartmoor, may also have been predicated on this connection between fairies, the dead, and corpse roads. She said it was a hot day and she became very weary as she toiled up the path toward the tor. Mac Manus takes up the story:

> She sat to rest on a "coffin" stone each time she came to one.
> The path is lined with large stones on either side, set at intervals
> up the steep incline . . . She was at least three-quarters of the
> way to the top when she saw a little man standing against one of
> the large boulders. He moved out from the rock and seemed to
> be watching her . . . She felt a little afraid because, while sitting
> on the various stones, she had wondered whether once people
> had lived on the moor and if they really had rested the coffins of
> their loved ones on the stones, and if so, whether this little man
> resented her using them as resting places too.[32]

The woman got to within 120 ft (37 m) of the little man and was able to obtain a good look at him – "It was no momentary sight, " she insisted. She said the figure was wearing a brown smock tied with a cord around the waist and his legs were covered with brown material. He was 3–4 ft (1–1.2 m) tall, and seemed elderly rather than young. The little figure disappeared, and when the woman got to the spot where he had been standing there was seemingly nowhere for anyone to hide.

So what was this? A hallucination caused by heat exhaustion? A tall tale? An actual paranormal event? Whatever, the account reflects the linkage between fairies and the dead through association with an old corpse road -a connection few are aware of.

As a footnote to this fairy-and-the-dead motif, it can be noted that one regional name for the fairy black dog is "barguest", and Sir Walter Scott felt this term derived from the German word *bahrgeist* meaning the spirit of the bier. This would make a definite link between the black dog, known to haunt old roads and lanes in general, and corpse roads in particular.

From Sea to Shining Sea?

It is difficult not to liken the lore concerning fairy paths and the placing of buildings in relation to them to the ideas surrounding the old Chinese landscape divination system *offeng shui,* in which houses and tombs had to be kept clear of straight roads and other straight features in the landscape for fear of interference by spirits passing along them. In Ireland, Britain, Holland, Germany, Russia, and even Albania, [33] land spirits and ghosts had special routes that it was dangerous for humans to obstruct. In fact, probably all the lands between China and Ireland had versions of such beliefs. Is it possible, then, that the same basic spirit-lore motif extended from one end of the landmass containing Asia and Europe to the other? It may be a heretical notion as far as mainstream scholarship is concerned, but there is subtle evidence nagging away in a number of contexts in addition to the startling similarities between the lore concerning fairy paths and *feng shui.*

Take, for example, the case of "Otzi", the deep-frozen Neolithic man found high in the Otztal Alps on the Italy-Austria border in September, 1991. His remains now lie in carefully controlled conditions in the South Tyrol Archaeological Museum in Bozen, Italy. This remarkably well-preserved survival from prehistory has supplied much fascinating information, but one particularly intriguing fact concerns his tattoos. These take the form of small dots arranged in linear groups either side of his lower spine, and on the right knee and both ankles, close to joints. X-rays showed bone degeneration in all these areas, and it seems likely that the tattoos were part of a pain-relieving treatment. The idea that tattooing can help in alleviating joint and muscle pains is old and widespread, being found in folk medicine traditions from the nomads of the Eurasian steppes to Tibet, and in ancient medical literature. In a fascinating parallel, another "ice man" was found preserved in a frozen tomb at Pazyryk in the Siberian Altai mountains. In addition to magnificent decorative tattoos, he also had a vertical line of pinpoint tattoo punctures on each side of his lumbar spine and an arc of pinpoints on the right ankle.[34] As this nomadic chieftain at Pazyryk belonged to the much later Iron Age period, it appears profoundly similar folk traditions could span thousands of years and thousands of miles. An intriguing additional factor is that the places on both the frozen bodies that had been tattooed with small dots *correspond to acupuncture points* and specifically those associated with the treatment of spinal deformation and joint pains.[35] It seems that this ancient and highly developed system of Chinese medicine was known to Stone Age Europeans.

Another fortuitous find – the Gundestrup Cauldron – similarly hints at a prehistoric traffic of ideas and beliefs across the continents of Asia and Europe. In 1891, peat cutters uncovered a silver vessel in a bog in Jutland, Denmark. The object, which is 27 in (69 cm) across, and over 15 in (38 cm) deep has been dated to the second century BC. Its sides are built up of plates decorated with hammered reliefs, which depict religious images and ritual scenes. These provide a rare snapshot of what was considered spiritually meaningful in northern Europe at that time, and it has provided interpretive headaches. The cauldron belongs to the pagan Celtic era, and some of its imagery does indeed depict objects known to belong to that time (such as animal-shaped trumpets known as *carnyxes)*, as well as figures who seem to relate to ancient Irish and Welsh mythology. Yet other images show Asiatic, and specifically Indian-like motifs. The cauldron was not a votive offering like those known to have been made by pagan Celts at lakes and bogs, because the area that became the Gundestrup bog had been dry land when the vessel was deposited or lost there. Further, this part of Denmark was not culturally part of the pagan Celtic European scene, being inhabited by Germanic peoples. Moreover, neither the European Celts nor Germanic societies carried out the type of silversmithing displayed on the vessel: analysis of the object suggests that the skills and influences that went into it came from as far eastwards as south-eastern Europe and the Black Sea region.

The workmanship of the vessel and the subject matter of some of its decoration seem at first glance to be at odds with its location. But archaeologist Tim Taylor has observed that the pan-Indo-European nature of the vessel's imagery, its craftsmanship, and the site of its discovery could be explained by known historical events and archaeological evidence. He draws attention to a depiction on the cauldron showing a human figure sprouting or wearing antlers, in the company of animals, seated in a yoga-like posture, and appearing to levitate (Figure 4).

Fig. 4. The mysterious horned figure on the Gundestrup Cauldron.

Taylor comments that this imagery, along with evidence from other sources, suggests "that druidism, steppe shamanism, and tantric yoga may have developed as interlinked systems of ritual specialization in the Eurasian later Iron Age".[36]

Yet another sign of an archaic trans-continental passage of ideas and beliefs can be found in the distribution of folklore motifs. Elsewhere I have given an account of Franz Boas, a noted late nineteenth- and early twentieth-century anthropologist who has studied American Indian societies, linguistics, legends, and traditions.[37] One of the links he noted was "a series of complicated tales" which were common to myths in both the Old and New Worlds. One example he gave was a fairy tale belonging to the Samoyed-speaking tribes of north-west Siberia. In this, two sisters were running from a pursuing cannibal witch. One girl threw a whetstone over her shoulder that transformed into a canyon, and so delayed the witch while she crossed the great divide. The witch had almost caught up with the two girls again when the other sister threw a flint over her shoulder. This transformed into a mountain, which blocked the witch's way completely. For good measure, the girl then threw a comb over her shoulder, which changed into a thicket. Boas found the virtually identical story among Indians of America's North Pacific coast: in this version, the child threw a whetstone which became a mountain, a bottle of oil which became a lake, and a comb which became a thicket. Boas felt that this motif had survived a five-thousand-mile migration journey to the Americas; what he did not know was that the recognisably same motif can be found far away in the other direction – in Wales to be precise. There, the foundation legend of the spa town of Llandrindod Wells tells of a man called Pengrych who snatches a beautiful maid from the clutches of three elves, who then pursue him. He has with him a bag of objects previously given to him by a mysterious old woman. As the first elf closes in on him Pengrych finds a lump of salt in the bag. He throws the salt over his shoulder at his pursuer, who promptly turns into a pool of water. Pengrych takes another object from the bag, a ball of sulphur, and throws that at the second elf, who also dissolves into a pool of water. Finally, as the third elf gets close, Pengrych fumbles for a chunk of iron in the bag – but drops it, so he turns and stabs the elf with an iron-bladed knife. The creature screams, falls to the ground and becomes a system of water spouts.[38]

A final observation relates specifically to an odd type of artefact. The American Indians have "dreamcatchers", which are hoops supporting a net of threads. These are made in order to snare evil spirits that can often approach a sleeping person. Usually, a small hole is left in the middle of the net to allow good dreams to reach the sleeper.

Travelling westward from the Americas to Tibet, we find a very similar tradition, one that is thought to date from pre-Buddhist times. It involves thread crosses *(mdos)* which were made as spirit traps.[39] These objects consisted of a pair of cross-sticks supporting coloured threads so that they were similar in appearance to a spider's web or even a modern radio antenna. They

Plate 5. A spirit trap fixed to a ceiling beam near the entrance door of a Bavarian house.

could be as much as 11 ft (3.3 m) across. Weather magicians used them to catch evil spirits flitting through the atmosphere. Others placed them on the roofs or at the entrances to dwellings to prevent the entry of unwanted spirits, and very large ones were used by monks to protect monasteries and their surrounding area from similar entities. Nepalese tribes deploy spirit traps of a similar nature to the Tibetan ones. Continuing westward to Europe, there existed a widespread tradition of making spirit traps that were also web-like features made of threads supported by hoops or cross-sticks. A trap might be large and placed on a staff to prevent ghosts passing along old paths, especially ones leading to or from cemeteries (therefore corpse roads), and might also have a protective rune emblazoned on it. Alternatively, a trap might be small and attached to a door frame or ceiling beam to protect a house from bad spirits coming in through the door from the dark night air outside (Plate 5).

These various examples seem to indicate that that there was conceptual traffic between Asia and Europe. But it might not be the case that it travelled from one or other end of the Eurasian landmass: genetic evidence indicates that early humanity as it emerged from Africa developed first in central Asia, so it could be that the ideas and concepts outlined above (and doubtless many more) spread out east and west from there. If that is true, though, it means that some of the spirit lore that has been examined in this and the previous chapter has very ancient origins indeed. Whatever the case may be, it is the contention in this book that subjects as apparently diverse as virtual spirit roads such as fairy paths, the German *Geisterwege* and the Dutch *Spokenwegen,* and the spirit lore attached to corpse roads, are all modified aspects of a deep substratum of spirit beliefs that once existed across the conjoined continents of Europe and Asia.

CHAPTER FOUR

Shamanic Routes

At locations throughout the Americas from Canada to Chile there are curious prehistoric markings emblazoned on the land: they take the form of images of animals, mythological creatures, and human figures, not to mention countless abstract and geometrical patterns. These markings are, variously, scratched into desert surfaces, or laid out in small stones, or sculpted into shaped earthen mounds. In addition, over a similar geographical distribution, there are areas where curious roads, paths or "lines" appear. These are not normal tracks or routes, and though they may have been used in some cases for everyday or military traffic, they also had deeper, religious and ceremonial meanings for the people who built and used them. Ancient American ceremonial routes were typically multi-functional, something that is rather alien to modern thought. I have described these enigmatic features at length elsewhere, [1] and here there is need to give only a basic overview of a selection of examples.

On the Road

The best-known mystery roads are the so-called "Nazca lines" in Peru. They are etched into desert tableland ("pampa") near Nazca, and share it with other kinds of markings depicting naturalistic images such as animals, reptiles, fish and flowers, and also geometric forms. The longest lines extend for 6 miles

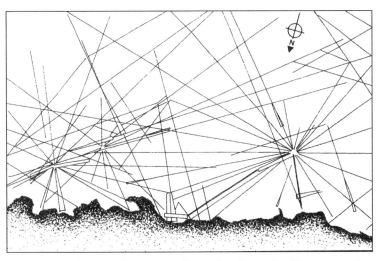

Fig. 5. Plan of some of the Nazca lines, showing a few "line centres".

57

(10 km) and are of varying widths. The network of lines seem to criss-cross the desert at random, but they meet or diverge at dozens of centres (usually low hillocks or mountain spurs), and at least one line from each links with another (Figure 5). The markings are thought to date from the Nazca culture of c.AD 600, but some markings may be older and some younger. Many of the lines at Nazca have deeply worn footpaths within them; the lines retain their almost Otherworldly geometric exactitude even though the ruts of these footpaths wander along inside them. Exactly where the paths are coming from or going to is not known.

There are smaller groups of similar lines scattered at other locations throughout the Peruvian Andes, and such features have puzzled investigators for decades. Astronomical theories have been put forward, but they are unconvincing. Other suggestions have been that the lines map water in the form of ancient aqueducts and arroyos (the dried beds of occasional streams), mark ancient cemeteries out on the pampa, or are ritual paths directed at holy, water-giving mountains – it is known that such mountains were regarded as actual gods in Andean cosmology. There is probably some truth in one or two of these ideas, but they do not seem to tell the whole story, nor explain the lines' distinctive straightness.

Far to the south of the Nazca markings, there are straight lines in the Atacama Desert of northern Chile, and hundreds of miles to the south-east there are networks of straight pathways on the altiplano of Bolivia. These Bolivian paths have been formed primarily by the clearance of vegetation and rocks along an exact straight course, along which are situated shrines and other holy places, *huacas*. Some of these features are 20 miles (32 km) in length – longer than anything at Nazca. Some do indeed go to mountain peaks, and Indians still process along some of them – literally in Indian file – to make offerings to the gods at the summits.

East of the Andes, hundreds of miles of mainly straight causeways are being found in various parts of the Amazon Basin. Archaeologist William Denevan points out that the "unusual straightness" of these rainforest roads is inexplicable in terms of utilitarian function, not to mention the difficulties the Indians must have experienced in laying them out in such an environment where the destination of a road was not visible. He remarks that they therefore take on "other significance".[2] That such significance is likely to have religious connotations is supported by the roads of the Kogi Indians of northern Colombia: the walking of their ancient stone paths is still today viewed by them as a religious observance, and this might also give a hint regarding the deeply-worn tracks within the Nazca lines.

Plate 6. Section of a restored sacbeob *or Mayan causeway at Chicken Itza, Mexico.*

In Central America, ancient and clearly ritual road systems have been found in Costa Rica (see Sampler entry 48), while in El Salvador, Honduras, Guatemala, Belize and south-east Mexico, the extensive domain of the ancient Maya, there are the remnants of broad causeways called *sacbeob* ("white ways") in the Mayan language running through the forest (see the Mexico section of the Sampler). These ran straight as arrows and used to link Mayan ceremonial cities as well as features such as plazas, temples and pyramids within them (Plate 6). Altars punctuated their courses. These causeways "facilitated the movement of its population for sacred, secular, and military purposes" says one of their keenest archaeological investigators, William Folan, acknowledging the multi-functional nature of ancient American Indian roads.[3] Further north in Mexico there are several straight causeway systems, in areas such as the Bajio, Rio Lajas, middle Lerma districts, and most importantly of all, around the archaeological site of La Quemada in Zacatecas (see Sampler entry 52). Roads at this latter location link ceremonial areas or radiate out to natural features such as caves or mountains. Archaeologist Charles Trombold has been making a special investigation of La Quemada for some decades. He has become convinced that the causeways were not ordinary roads but had to be associated with ritual or ceremonial activities. Up near Mexico's modern border with the United States, in the Chihuahua Desert, vestiges of similar ceremonial roads have been noted around the archaeological site of Casas Grande, though these have not yet been investigated in any great detail.

In the United States itself, the bulk of known ancient ceremonial and ritual road systems appear to be in California and the Southwestern states. The Miwok Indians used unusual trails in the California sierras:

> Many trails were wide and worn a couple of feet deep from long use. They could be traced long after the Indians had gone and the paths were abandoned. They seem to have gone in straight lines . . . without detouring for mountains in the way . . . Trails were marked in various ways . . . Sometimes piles of twigs or cairns of stone along a trail have been called markers.[4]

Other archaeologists also noted the straightness of these ancient tracks: "Miwok trails were usually almost airline in their directness, running up hill and down dale without zigzags or detours".[5] In the Colorado Desert, in the extreme south-east of California, there are some curious trails only 6–12 in (15–30 cm) in width, and usually two or more of them run in parallel. In some cases, small stones were used to edge the trails, and at intervals they are punctuated with cairns. The largest of these cairns – its collection of stones is estimated to weigh 3 tons – is to be found at the top of the Mopi Pass in the Turtle Mountains of San Bernadino County. These trails were used by the Yuman Indians but it is very possible they were re-using even older tracks.[6] There are also short but distinctive ritual trails in Death Valley, California, which belonged to the Shoshone or their predecessors (see Sampler entry 53). Remnants of similar ancient Indian trails have been found in Arizona, especially along the Gila River Valley, and likewise in Nevada. There are some segments of ancient roads surviving in Colorado – one near Boulder Pass, 55 miles (88.5 km) west of Denver, traverses a plateau at an altitude of over 11,000 ft (3, 353 m) above sea level. In 1878, it was described as "an old roadway which has evidently borne infinite travel of some kind".[7]

Not thought to be related to these trails are the remarkable ceremonial roads around Chaco Canyon in New Mexico, a ritual centre of the lost civilization of the Anasazi Indians (Plate 7). The roads are broad, engineered features, some running in parallel like the much narrower trails of California's Colorado Desert (above), and are now thought to have extended across the whole Four Corners region, where New Mexico, Colorado, Utah and Arizona meet. "The most common feature of the Chaco roads is their straight-line course, which is maintained in spite of topographic obstacles, " states NASA

Plate 7. The ruins of a ceremonial "Great House" on the floor of Chaco Canyon, New Mexico, with the north wall of the canyon beyond.

archaeologist Thomas Sever, who has made aerial studies of them. He noted that the Anasazi road makers were not efficient in any modern sense, deliberately taking their roads straight through or over topographical obstacles.[8] (See Sampler entries 54 and 55 for a more detailed exploration of Anasazi roads).

A few unusual ancient roads are known of elsewhere in the United States, especially with regard to the two-thousand-year-old Hopewell Indian culture of the Ohio Valley. The longest of these so far identified is a dead-straight sixty-mile-long example in Ohio connecting the Hopewell ceremonial centres of Newark, a complex of gigantic geometric earthworks covering many acres, to the necropolis known as Mound City at Chillicothe. The faint fragments disclosing its course have been pieced together by means of standard and infrared aerial photography and ground investigation by various researchers at different times.[9]

Deep Foundations

So what were these unusual ancient roads all about? The late John Hyslop of the Museum of Natural History in New York, an experienced field investigator of prehistoric Andean road systems, considered that roads constructed in extraordinary ways are most likely related to ritual or symbolic concerns. He urged researchers to realize that prehistoric American Indian roads had meanings and uses unfamiliar to our understanding of roads, concepts that had religious, sacred or mythological connotations. They could not be interpreted in "purely materialistic terms".[10]

A clue to the puzzle must surely lie with the common distinguishing feature of the old roads – their straightness. As archaeologist Charles Trombold confirms: "If there is one attribute that characterizes New World road systems it is straightness."[11] While not all the old American routes were always completely straight, this is nevertheless the prevailing attribute that persists, irrespective of the time period, the culture involved, or a route's location within the Americas. It was not just a case of straight roads being laid on deserts and other flat areas, they occur also in mountainous regions and rainforests. As I have written elsewhere, we have to follow the common denominator of their straightness and not be diverted by cultures, chronologies, or types of feature.[12] Whether the routes were just "lines", pathways marked simply on the ground, or had evolved into substantial, engineered structures such as causeways in the more complex Indian cultures, the spirit of the strange straightness haunted them all – that same quality, it has to be said, present in the Old World's spirit ways, especially the invisible, "virtual" ones.

So, why so straight? At one level, it could be a symbolic attribute of Otherworld roads. "The cultural ordering which opposes the wild is a linear ordering, " British archaeologist Ian Hodder has perceptively pointed out in another but not totally unrelated context.[13] But in prehistoric America this probably came about as a result of stimuli emerging from a deeper source than mere intellectual symbolical conceptualization. That the deep source was *shamanism* is fairly certain. This is supported by the fact that virtually all known straight road and "line" features are located in the territories of peoples known to have practised shamanism and were built and used at the height of those cultures. The Hopewell culture, for instance, was a collection of tribes that subscribed to a specific shamanically-based religion. Even complex and hierarchical state-like cultures such as that of the Maya were ruled by shaman-priests – the surviving Maya still practise shamanism today.[14]

Then there is the rock art connection. Some of the roads and ground figures occur in areas where prehistoric rock art sites are common, and these locations were where shamans held their vision quests and interacted with the spirit world. Much of the content of the carved or painted rock art imagery is thought to relate to visions seen during trance – altered mind states often engendered by drugs. Various hallucinogenic substances were used by different ancient Indian peoples: the most prevalent included the mescaline-containing peyote or san pedro cacti, the Datura-based jimson weed, hallucinogenic mushrooms, and *ayahuasca,* an infusion based on a mind-altering vine that is still used by some Amazon tribes. Many dozens of other hallucinogenic substances, in the form of seeds, herbs, beans, and even massive doses of tobacco, were also pressed into service by the vision-hungry Indians. There are two broad categories of rock art imagery associated with trances. The first involves winged figures, because entranced states (especially those provoked by hallucinogens) typically produce a sense of spirit or out-of-body flight – the so-called "aerial journey" of the shaman when in his entranced ecstatic state. The second is a range of geometric imagery that is typical of the earlier stages of trance (again, especially drug-induced) that is thought to be caused by "hard-wired" neurophysiological factors in the visual cortex. These latter types of mental patterns are called "entoptic". Both effects – the sensation of flight and geometrical visions – are universal and so occur across all shamanistic societies all over the world. However, the meaning ascribed to the geometric imagery can be culture-specific, and so may vary.[15]

These same basic imagery elements are recognizable in the much larger scale figurative ground markings. They could be there in the straight road/line systems, too, if less obviously so: Jay von Werlhof tellingly notes that the Mojave Indians treat both figurative ground markings and sacred trails as having been made by the same spirit creators.[16] The shamanic "flight" sensation might have been expressed metaphorically in the straight line ("as the crow flies", "straight as an arrow"), underpinned by the ecstatic or out-of-body sensation at the heart of the shamanic experience. This was first suggested by anthropologists in 1977, when Marlene Dobkin de Rios argued that both the figurative and linear markings at Nazca and elsewhere were made to be comprehensible only from the air because entranced shamans were believed literally to fly on their aerial journey to the spirit world.[17] They were sacred landmarks laminated onto the physical topography, guiding the out-of-body shaman or acting as signs of power to deter enemy shamans and sorcerers, for there were frequent magical battles between shamans of different tribes). Dobkin de Rios suggested that the linear patterns related to entoptic imagery. In this view, the straight line, that deep foundation of the straight ceremonial roads, was symbolic of the experience of leaving the body, quite apart from being a distinctive expression of supernatural power.

In modern accounts of out-of-body and near-death experiences, the image of floating down a tunnel is often described – this is, in fact, an entoptic effect. The argument is that prehistoric American Indians chose to represent the same effect on the ground as a straight line. This image of straightness may have evolved so that it was first symbolic of the esoteric experience of shamanism, and then became associated with rote religious observance, then with shaman-chieftains, and ultimately with divine kingship and its accoutrements, including military rule and ceremonial display – the ancient

Americas were as prone to being ruled by divine kings as was the Old World.

Ghost Roads

There is another strand of ethnological evidence that adds a telling dimension to this Otherworldly approach to the mystery of the ancient lines and roads. It indicates that certain ancient American societies complemented their physical road systems with invisible, spectral ones. Kogi shamans *(mamas)* of Colombia, for instance, claim to travel their often straight, stone-paved roads in their trances, because they are deemed to be the traces of spirit paths in the Otherworld. With their entranced eyes the Kogi shamans can see spirit paths continuing straight on beyond where the physical paths terminate (Figure 6).[18]

Fig. 6. The lines carved on this "map stone" in Kogi Indian territory, Colombia, apparently depict the Kogi's special roads, both visible and invisible. (After a photograph by Alan Ereira)

The implication is that the physical roads are merely the visible part of a more comprehensive but invisible system of spirit routes. This is spelled out directly in Mayan tradition, which states that in addition to the visible causeways, the *sacbeob*, there are invisible ones that run underground (possibly connecting the mysterious ballcourts found in the ancient Mayan cities) and through the air – these are called *Kusan Sum*. One of these aerial routes is said to run between the ancient Mayan cities of Dzibilchaltan and Izamal on the Yucatan peninsula. Another example is described in Sampler entry 49. In the southwest of the United States, information collected in the late nineteenth century from aged Indian shamans (referred to as "doctors") tells that certain hill summits and mountain peaks were venerated as holy places where great supernatural power resided. These were supposedly connected by invisible threads or cobwebs stretching through the air. Shamans seeking supernatural power travelled along these routes during their "dreams" (trances).[19] The San Francisco Peak near Flagstaff was just one of the sacred summits connected by this invisible network, which was perceived as extending over an area 500 miles (800 km) across. At least one ancient straight line etched on a mesa top in the Gila River Valley seems related to this belief in spirit travel by means of invisible threads.[20]

It is beginning to look as if the physical roads, paths and "lines" of prehistoric America were just a partial, visible expression of a more complex conceptual geography of the Otherworld that was curiously widespread among ancient American Indians.

CHAPTER FIVE

Stone-Age Spirit Ways?

There is usually some form of documentation or anthropological information associated with most kinds of Otherworldly routes that helps us to come to a conclusion about their nature. But when we come to the "deep time" of the Stone Age, we have nothing but the features themselves and have to rely on whatever archaeological and interpretative information can be gleaned from them. Here we look at the main types of Old World prehistoric linear feature that fall into the category of possible Otherworldly routes.

Avenues

A number of major Neolithic sites have "avenues" connected to them, including the most famous of them all – Stonehenge. There, the traces of an earthen avenue formed by parallel ditches have been found to the north-east, beyond Stonehenge's outlying Heel Stone, extending the main (midsummer

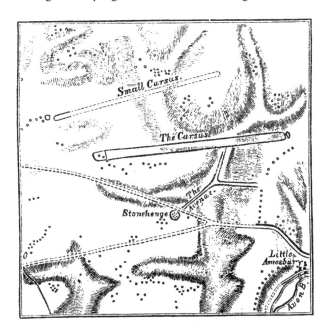

Fig. 7. This old plan of Stonehenge and its surroundings
shows a northerly extension of the Stonehenge Avenue,
and the linear earthwork known as the cursus.
(J Fergusson, Rude Stone Monuments, 1871)

Plate 8. Looking north along the West Kennet Avenue, Avebury.

sunrise) axis of the actual Stonehenge monument into the surroundings. It is perfectly straight but after about 1500 ft (460 m) it makes a sudden turn to the east. (Intriguingly, an aerial archaeologist mentioned to me that once when flying over the site just after sunrise he glimpsed glittering lines of dewdrops extending in a straight line beyond the bend in the avenue. He thought this might possibly indicate soil disturbance relating to an earlier course, showing that the feature had continued straight on.) Interestingly, some early plans of the site show this continuation (Figure 7).

Another example of a prehistoric avenue has been found at Godmanchester near Cambridge. At this site a 2-mile (3-km) long earthen avenue leads to what had been a Neolithic timber circle rather than a stone circle. Burials were found along the course of the avenue.

The purposes of Stone Age avenues are not known, but a ceremonial function is usually assumed. This might be too simplistic, though, as is indicated at Avebury, the world's largest stone circle, set within a circular earthen ditch and bank forming a henge, which is located 20 miles (32 km) north of Stonehenge. This great ring of stones had two avenues of standing stones connected to it. One, the almost destroyed Beckhampton Avenue, extends to (or comes in from) the west. The other, the West Kennet Avenue, connects to the southern edge of the henge. Its full length was 1½ miles (2.5 km) and it connected the hilltop site known as the Sanctuary with Avebury henge itself. Only a segment, near the henge, is now visible where fallen stones have been re-erected or missing stones have been replaced by concrete plinths marking the places where they once stood (Plate 8). All that is visible today at the Sanctuary are concentric rings of concrete plinths marking post and stone holes. The place was once a sequence of (probably roofed) timber structures, and these were finally embraced by a stone circle. The remains of this was destroyed in the eighteenth century by local farmers. Bones and evidence of feasts were unearthed at the site, and it is generally interpreted as having been a mortuary house where ritual or ceremonial activities took place. It is thought by many archaeologists that a body would have been rested there before being carried in solemn procession along the avenue, through a huge timber enclosure (whose remains have only recently been discovered) and on to the henge.

From the timber enclosure, the course of the avenue seems to take a sinuous route northward to the henge and stone ring. In fact, the two lines of stones forming the avenue are made up of several discrete straight sections. Burials and votive offerings were placed at the points where the sections changed direction. But was this avenue really used as a ceremonial way for major processions of people, perhaps conveying their dead chieftains to their final resting place? Perhaps not, because research using geophysical techniques has thrown up a startling finding: the ground was as compacted *outside* the two lines of stones as inside.[1] It appears large groups of people (or smaller groups more frequently) trod the ground along the *edges* of West Kennet Avenue. If people moved along the sides of the avenue, it could be that the interior was reserved just for a few officiants carrying the bones of the dead ancestor (perhaps as a periodic ceremonial display rather than for burial). Alternatively, perhaps the avenue was deemed to be solely for the passage of the spirit issuing from the corpse that was being subjected to ritual inside the Sanctuary. In which case, West Kennet would have been primarily a *spirit way* rather than a processional way for living human beings.[2]

Could the precursors of the spirit beliefs that attached themselves to the medieval corpse roads have originated as far back as the Stone Age? Such a suggestion has to be speculation because we simply do not know what happened at Avebury, but it *is* fairly clear that West Kennet Avenue, with its peripheral burials and linkage to a probable charnel house, was a death road of some kind, as, possibly, were many of the other Stone Age avenues.

Cursuses

A "cursus" is a type of linear earthwork, an earthen avenue usually defined by ditches and internal banks, and almost always having closed ends. It can therefore be described as a very elongated enclosure. But there can be variations on this basic form. Some cursuses were outlined by pits or postholes rather than ditches, and cursus lengths can vary from a few hundred yards (metres) to 1 mile (1.6 km) or more. The rather curious name for this type of monument means "racecourse" in Latin. The name was originally attributed to the nearly 2-mile (3-km) long feature just north of Stonehenge by the antiquarian

William Stukeley in 1723 because he thought the feature was a Roman racetrack. Similarly, later in the same century, a Roman origin was assumed for Cleaven Dyke in Perthshire, Scotland, now also recognized as being a cursus. In fact, archaeologists now know the monument type dates to the Neolithic era.

Most cursus monuments have been ploughed out and so are difficult to see at ground level, only being visible as crop marks when viewed from the air. Approximately one hundred have now been identified in Britain, and are to be found throughout the land, with concentrations in southern England, the Midlands, lowland Scotland, and eastern mid-Wales. Important examples include, among many others, the Stonehenge Cursus already mentioned (see Figure 7), the Dorset cursus – really two cursuses butted end-to-end and extending in all for about 6 miles (10 km), the mile-long Scorton Cursus in Yorkshire, the Drayton Cursus, also 1 mile (1.5 km) long, in Oxfordshire, and a cursus running for 2 miles (3 km) immediately to the west of Heathrow airport, London. A cursus is usually fairly straight, sometimes exactingly so, or straight in sections, and it is this regularity that is a key identifying characteristic of the monument type. Nevertheless, there are cursuses with sinuous or crooked sections, or slightly curved sides.

Four possible cursuses have also been identified in Ireland: on the Hill of Tara; below the Loughcrew Hills, on which over twenty chambered cairns are placed; the "Knockauns" at Teltown, and immediately to the north-east of Newgrange. There are, additionally, groups of linear earthworks in northern France and Brittany that may come within the definition of this monument type.

Despite being among the largest monuments produced in the Stone Age, the function of cursuses remains a mystery. Probably because they represent such an interpretative challenge, serious archaeological investigation has been scant until the last two decades of the twentieth century, when cursuses began to be studied with more vigour. Although excavation has revealed evidence of postholes, cremations, inner mounds and other signs of ritual activity within some cursuses, for the most part they seem to have been rather empty features. Yet they were clearly of importance to the Stone Age people who built them, so what could they have been for?

First, what do we actually *know* about cursuses, apart from their groundplans? One pattern associated with these locations is that most are situated close to rivers. Further, a particular type of prehistoric pottery called Peterborough Ware has been found in some cursuses as well as in river deposits or offerings. Another angle is how some cursuses appear to refer to their natural surroundings. The Stonehenge Cursus, for example, aligns with a point on a distinctive ridge on the eastern horizon called Beacon Hill, a name that underlines its visibility.[3] Cleaven Dyke aligns with the Hill of Lethendy to its north-west. The cursus at Dorchester-on-Thames lies beneath the prominent Sinoden Hills, which rise distinctively from the floodplain of the River Thames and are the kind of twin, rounded hills reminiscent of breasts that ancient people usually regarded as symbolic of a fertility, or Earth, goddess.[4] A third, key, factor about cursuses is that they are typically part of ceremonial landscapes - they are often placed in association with other monuments such as henges, and they almost invariably link or

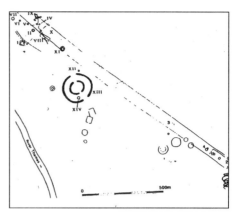

Fig. 8. Plan of the Dorchester-on-Thames cursus and associated earthworks. The large concentric circles represent a henge monument, while the smaller circular and other features represent various prehistoric burial mounds. (After Roy Loveday, 1999).

pass through areas containing burial mounds or other prehistoric places of burial (Figure 8). Finally, there is another characteristic frequently present, namely that the axes of some cursuses align with prehistoric monuments beyond their ends. The axis of the Stonehenge cursus, for instance, not only points to Beacon Hill on the eastern skyline but, before that, aligns with a standing stone named the Cuckoo Stone and on through a henge monument known as Woodhenge (Figure 9). A large percentage of cursuses also point to medieval churches; why this should be so is problematical, there being thousands of years between cursuses and churches, unless the churches now occupy places that had significance in prehistoric times.[5]

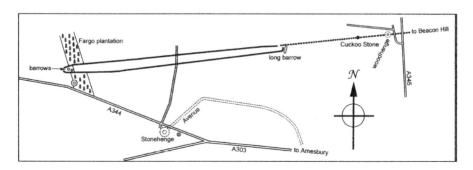

Fig. 9. Plan of the nearly 2-mile (3-km) long Stonehenge Cursus, with dotted line indicating the extension of the cursus axis through the Cuckoo Stone and Woodhenge.

So what theories have developed about the function of cursuses? As with avenues, it has been widely assumed that they were associated with processional activities of some kind. It has therefore been suggested that there may have been a symbolic link between the flow of the associated (and presumably venerated) river with a given cursus and processional movement within it.[6] Another suggestion is that cursuses were ritual paths. A variant on this idea is that cursuses marked where such a holy or ceremonial way had existed – the monumentalization of a route.[7] It has also been suggested that the linear monuments allowed for a formalized form of pilgrimage.

The problem with such interpretations is that cursuses are not through ways; they are enclosures, however elongated they may be. It could be that the assumption of physical processional activity being the purpose of cursuses is misguided, as could be the case with prehistoric avenues. One thing that seems certain is that cursuses are funerary in nature, given their association with places of burial: could it therefore be that their perceived function was to do with *spirits*? It has been noted in previous chapters that the idea of spirits of various kinds moving through the landscape was a belief held almost universally in ancient times. Perhaps cursuses were reserves where the spirits of the buried ancestors could be summoned by ritualistic performances and allowed to move between burial sites. Because spirits were thought of as being potentially dangerous, such activity took place within defined, probably sanctified enclosures, much as today we place dangerous animals in zoo enclosures while giving them as much room for movement as possible. Rituals involved in raising the ancestral spirits might have been the Stone Age equivalent of today's nuclear technology. If something like this was the case, then a cursus was a *cordon sanitaire* placed around a ritual interaction with ancestral spirits. This could also explain the placing of cursuses next to rivers – there was an almost universal and abiding belief of great antiquity that spirits cannot cross flowing water, and that rivers were boundaries between the realms of the living and the dead.[8] In previous chapters we encountered this belief in the customs associated with the carriage of corpses to burial and with the believed movement of fairies. Perhaps, like the Stone-Age avenue, the cursus was the prototype of the medieval corpse road.

Stone rows

Stone rows are another form of linear prehistoric monument, belonging to the late Neolithic or early Bronze Age periods. Like avenues and cursuses, stone rows – in Britain at least – tend to pass through or link burial sites, and could be a variant of the same concept.

Stone alignments occur in several parts of the Old World, especially in South-East Asia, but the greatest concentration of stone rows or alignments is in the Carnac-Ville region of Brittany. Here, complexes of multiple stone rows stride across the landscape, ranging from dumpy rocks to massive megaliths. The major groupings include Kerlescan, north-east of Carnac-Ville, made up of thirteen main stone rows running in parallel for over 1000 ft (300 m); Kermario, north-north-east of Carnac-Ville, comprises seven main lines of stones; Kerzerho, between Erdeven and Plouharnel, is the remnant of ten alignments that originally extended for over 1 mile (1.5 km); Menec, northwest of Carnac-Ville, consists of twelve rows of stones running for ½ mile (800 m) between two cromlechs (burial sites); Petite-Menec, 2½ miles (4 km) north-east of Carnac-Ville, made up of eight irregular lines of stones; and St Barbe, Plouharnel, the remnant of stone alignments once extending for over 1200 ft (370 m).

Short stone rows occur in and around Fermanagh, Northern Ireland, and in the south-west of the Irish Republic. In Britain, stone rows are prevalent in numerous moorland and mountainous locations. Among other examples, Scotland has a curious fan-arrangement of 22 rows at the Hill O' Many Stanes near Wick, and in Wales a notable example is the line of tall stones near Fishguard known as Parc-y-Meirw. In England, stone rows are to be found (and are still being discovered) on moorland areas in Yorkshire, the Pennines, and in the southwestern counties of Cornwall and Devon. The greatest number, over sixty surviving stone rows, exist on Devon's granite upland of Dartmoor, where many more examples have been destroyed or lost (Plate 9). The surviving rows occur in single, double, and multiple configurations, and range in length between a few hundred

Plate 9. The eastern end of a double stone row at Merrivale, Dartmoor. Note the triangular "blocking stone" (see Sampler entry 10).

yards (metres) and 2 miles (3 km). Very little detailed archaeological investigation has been carried out other than locating them precisely and describing their appearance. What limited excavation has been conducted has revealed virtually no information.

The recurring pattern seems to be the association of stone rows with places of interment, as was the case with cursuses. Are we again dealing with monumentalized spirit tracks related to the dead ancestors? Such an idea is strengthened by the curious fact that many stone rows have "blocking stones" at one or both ends. These are distinctive stones set at right angles to the axis of the row – as if preventing "something" from escaping into the landscape at large. As with the case of fairy paths (Chapter Three), there is a hint here of a trans-Eurasian belief in the control of spirit movement, as exemplified by Chinese *feng-shui*.

PART TWO

FOREGROUND

A Sampler of Otherworldly Routes

NOTES

The Sampler is divided into two main parts: the first gives examples of OLD WORLD routes in Britain, Germany, Ireland and the Netherlands, the second gives examples of NEW WORLD routes in Australia, Costa Rica, Mexico and the United States.

PURPOSES OF THE SAMPLER – As mentioned in the Introduction, the primary purpose of this Sampler is to put "flesh on the bones" of the background chapters in Part One. The Sampler entries in the following pages provide detailed descriptions of various kinds of physical routes that have Otherworld connotations, allowing the reader to obtain a better sense of the nature of such features and a firmer grasp of the lore concerning them. The secondary purpose of the Sampler is to encourage visits to some of the examples described so as to allow the reader to gain a direct, "hands on" appreciation of the various kinds of physical vestiges of a fast-disappearing heritage, an ancient psychogeography that was a form of land-based spirituality. For that reason, most of the entries describe routes meant to be walked or visited. Some of the routes, though, are unsuitable for this, as will be apparent from the entries concerned, and have been included simply for information.

SCOPE OF SAMPLER – Please note that this is only a sampler, and not a gazetteer. It represents just a sample of Otherworldly routes in selected countries.

MAPS & DIRECTIONS – At the beginning of each entry there are directions to the location involved, giving a general geographic "fix" of the area concerned, and in most cases this will be adequate for visiting the features described when used in conjunction with a good quality tourist or road map. In some cases, though, a more detailed map will be necessary, and this will become apparent in the entries concerned. Large-scale Ordnance Survey (O.S.) maps were used for fieldwork for the British and Irish entries, so map grid references are additionally given in these cases for those who wish to use them. (For anyone wanting to know about grid references, please see the Appendix.) The types of Ordnance Survey maps variously referred to in the British and Irish sections of the Sampler are as follows:

LANDRANGER – These are the standard British 1:50,000-scale maps (equivalent to 1¼ in or 3.75 cm to the mile). They contain a wealth of detail – more than enough for most purposes. Note that there are various editions of Landranger maps in circulation.

OUTDOOR LEISURE/EXPLORER – 1:25,000-scale maps (equivalent to 2½ in or 6.25 cm to the mile) covering specific and usually quite large areas, principally National Parks and other regions of outstanding beauty. These give highly detailed information, such as the names of some roads, field boundaries, and more detailed footpath information than on the Landranger maps.

PATHFINDER – These are another, older type of 1:25,000-scale maps covering smaller areas, but the whole country is mapped by this series.

DISCOVERY SERIES – These are the Irish O.S. 1:50,000 maps, which can be bought directly from the appropriate Ordnance Survey offices via the Internet (for example, www.ordnancesurvey.co.uk), or through specialist map shops (such as Stanfords in London and Bristol, or the Map Centre in London). A range of local O.S. maps are usually stocked by good newsagents and bookshops in any given area.

SAMPLER ENTRIES – (i) Entries describe actual routes or specific sites where issues related to Otherworldly routes can be illustrated.
(ii) Entries are numbered consecutively throughout the Sampler, irrespective of country, to make for easier reference.
(iii) Most of the entries described in the Sampler have been field researched by me, but a small number have not. An asterisk* denotes those entries where I have relied on the fieldwork of others.

RIGHTS OF WAY – Although most of the footpaths described are public rights of way, this might not always be the case and right of way should not be assumed. Ask locally when in doubt.

CHANGES – Please be aware that some details on the ground concerning the routes themselves or directions to them may have changed since the fieldwork for the Sampler was undertaken.

COUNTRY CODE – This is the code of conduct expected of all visitors to the countryside and requires that everyone ensure they leave field gates as they are found, open or closed, and not to drop litter, light fires (except in officially designated places), cause damage, trespass, or make loud noises that might frighten animals.

OLD WORLD

ENGLAND
Corpse Roads, Churchways, and Spirit Routes

CORNWALL

● 1. LUDGVAN

Pathfinder 1:25,000 O.S. map no.1364 ("St Ives & Penzance [North]"). Ludgvan is a village about 3 miles (5 km) north-east of the town of Penzance (situated on the south coast of Cornwall's Land's End – Penwith – district, near the end of the peninsula) and can be approached from the A30 at Crowlas by taking the B3309 road. Trezelah is a hamlet 2 miles (3 km) north of Penzance and 2 miles (3 km) west of Ludgvan, and Gulval is a village 1 mile (1.5 km) east of Penzance and 2 miles (3 km) south of Trezelah.

Ludgvan and Trezelah share a curious relationship in a rather specific piece of old local folklore that relates to the divinatory practices associated with corpse ways. The folktale, taken directly from oral sources in the nineteenth century, tells of a widow who had lived in the hamlet of Trezelah (SW 477.336) a century earlier. Trezelah was first documented in 1284, and consists of a small cluster of granite houses.

The widow was out walking with a friend when she saw a strange spotted dog that seemed to know her but was invisible to the friend. It transformed into the ghost of her husband, and he told her to wait for him at a given time outside her house. She duly waited, and her husband appeared on cue. Picking her up in his arms he "carried her over the tree-tops as far as Ludgvan Church, where he deposited her on the Church-stile, from whence she saw a great many spirits, some good and some bad".[1] The bad spirits wanted her to go with them, but the woman's husband told her to stay where she was. Other spirits came by and gave her information that would help her to regain her rights, which had been appropriated by others after her husband's death. The widow was borne back through the air by her husband's spirit "by the way they had come", losing a shoe in a tree's topmost branches on the way. Before he left her, the husband said, "I must take something from you; either your eyesight, or your hearing". She preferred deafness to blindness, and from that hour could never hear a word.

Ludgvan (pronounced "Lujjen") has had a church on the present site for over a thousand years – a seventh-century grave marker stone was unearthed in the churchyard in 1962. The present structure (SW 505.331) is somewhat less ancient, though, the chancel dates from the fourteenth century and there

Plate 10. Ludgvan church stile.

have been various additions, such as the tower and northern aisle, and sundry restorations in subsequent centuries. The church stile still exists (Plate 10), located a few hundred yards from the church itself at SW 5062.3300, and is at the end of a well-preserved churchway leading from the hamlet of Ludgvan Leaze half a mile (0.8 km) to the south. The clear implication of the folktale is that spirits passed along this path and a seer at the stile could interrogate them – the ancient art of stile divination. The survival of the folktale gives us a rare opportunity to identify an actual stile that was used for this practice.

Other possible Cornish divination stiles mentioned in folklore include a certain "White Stile" on the old corpse way from Carharrack to Gwennap, to the south-east of Redruth, a town 17 miles (27 km) east of Penzance. Possibly fashioned from an old cross, this stile was feared locally as being haunted by a ghost. Also, folklore recorded directly from oral tradition by the eighteenth-century Cornish antiquarian, W. Bottrell, tells of a specific "church-way stile" near the hamlet of Brea (SW 3788.2802), close to Land's End, that was haunted by fairies. It was said to be where they left a changeling (a "changeling" being a replacement that fairies left in exchange for an abducted human child).

●2. BOSULLOW to MADRON

Pathfinder 1:25,000 O.S. map no.1364 ("St Ives & Penzance [North]"). Bosullow Common is 4 miles (6.5 km) north-west of Penzance and the village of Madron is located 1 mile (1.5 km) north-west of the town.

The Cornish liked a "good buryin'", and walking funerals were common in Penwith until the beginning of the twentieth century. Typically, a coffin would be preceded by a double row of singers and followed by the mourners, perhaps fifty or more arranged as men and women in couples. Accompanying the coffin – "walking next the corpse" – would be the closest relatives of the dead person. The leader of the singers would read out a hymn two lines at a time, and the cortege would sing them slowly and solemnly to well-known "buryin' tunes".[2] Speaking with elderly people in 1992, local researchers Gabrielle

Hawkes and Tom Henderson-Smith were told that because the processions were usually so long the system would often break down and people at the back of the cortege could find themselves singing a different hymn from those at the front! As well as resting and singing at selected crosses along the way, the bearers would use granite blocks next to certain stiles for the same purpose.

Because there are numerous farmsteads and hamlets in the Bosullow Common area, there were fairly regular walking funerals carried out from there to the appropriate churchtown, Madron, 3 miles (5 km) distant. Most of the course of this churchway is now appropriated by the motor road that joins Penzance with the north Cornish coast, but on the approach to Madron the original churchway kept straight where the road now deviates. The course of this final straight mile (1.6 km) or so (extending from SW 4345.3338 to SW 4495.3210) can now be traced as a series of footpath and narrow lane segments and has a surviving wayside cross at SW 4452.3254. This distinct linearity perhaps explains why churchways used as corpse roads were known locally in Penwith as "coffin lines".[3]

An interesting feature of this churchway is that it passes close by the Neolithic dolmen of Lanyon Quoit (Figure 10), at SW 4295.3370 – indeed, if the road did not make a sharp, dog-leg bend at this point the route would go right through the monument. (Perhaps not surprisingly, there are accounts of ghostly encounters near the quoit.) It makes one wonder about the true age of the routes followed by some of the churchways in this district: are they Christian versions of prehistoric ways of the dead?[4] (I was first made aware of this churchway route by the work of Gabrielle Hawkes and Tom Henderson-Smith.)

Fig. 10. The Cornish dolmen known as Lanyon Quoit. (J T Blight)

●3. ST LEVAN

Pathfinder 1:25,000 O.S. map no. 1368 ("Land's End & Newlyn"). The tiny village of St Levan lies close to the south coast of the Land's End peninsula, about 7 miles (11 km) west of Penzance as the crow flies. It is at the end of a narrow country lane that leaves the B3315 at Trethewey and passes through Porthcurno.

Several churchways converge on St Levan's church (SW 381.223), one of the most dramatic being the corpse way that comes to it from Bodellan and

Porthcurno to the east, especially the last stretch from the ancient farmstead of Rospletha (SW 383.224). This runs straight toward the church and is marked by a wayside Celtic cross (Plate 11). This segment is known in local lore as "St Levan's Path", and the claim is that it was used by the Dark Ages saint to walk from his dwelling at Bodellan to his chapel on the cliff edge overlooking the cove of Porth Chapel, very close to the present site of the medieval church, from where he would fish. Tradition has it that every time the saint walked along the path the grass grew greener behind his footsteps than anywhere else in the field. There is also a legend that one Sunday a woman called Johanna, who lived at Rospletha, rebuked the saint as he passed by for going fishing on the Sabbath.

Plate 11. St Levan's Path, looking toward the church. The upright object in the foreground on the right side of the churchway is an old Cornish waymarker cross.

The path comes to a wooden stile, then continues on a short distance to the edge of the churchyard where there is a granite stile, another cross, and a resting

Plate 12. The full-size coffin stone on the boundary of St Levan's churchyard.

stone the shape and size of a coffin (Plate 12). This corpse way was the first I deliberately researched, and I was surprised and delighted to find this rare survival of a coffin stone: it certainly removed any doubt as to the nature of the path.

The coffin stone is on the boundary of the churchyard, which is an ancient *llan*, a sacred enclosure certainly older than the church itself and probably pre-Christian. What made

Fig. 11. A 19th-century drawing of St Levan's church, Land's End, Cornwall. The split rock is on the right of the picture in the churchyard, and the Celtic cross stands by the entrance path to the church. The churchyard now has many graves within it. (J T Blight)

this a holy site is undoubtedly the distinctive split boulder now surrounded by graves (Figure 11). That it had pagan significance is indicated by the fact that a tall Celtic cross is placed immediately alongside it, as if to "Christianize" the feature. This split rock is, naturally enough, known as St Levan's Stone, and a tradition states that it was created by a blow from the saint's fist. According to local folklore it was venerated in Arthurian times, and Merlin is supposed to have predicted:

> *When with panniers astride,*
> *A pack-horse can ride*
> *Through St Levan's Stone,*
> *The world will be done.*

The good news is that the split is still far too narrow to admit a laden pack-horse.

●4. WICCA to ZENNOR

Pathfinder 1:25,000 O.S. map no.1364 ("St Ives & Penzance [North]"). Zennor village lies near the north coast of the Land's End peninsula 4 miles (6.5 km) west of St Ives, on the B3306 road.

This churchway runs for over 1 mile (1.5 km) westward from the

Plate 13. Looking toward Zennor church, Cornwall, from a granite stile on the churchway.

farmstead of Wicca (SW 472.395) to Zennor, paralleling the coast. It was marked by at least five known stone crosses or inscribed stones, a few of which survive. "Earlier still, it may have been marked by menhirs (individual standing stones), at least three of which existed along the way, " observes local historian, Craig Weatherhill. It passes through small stone-walled fields that were first laid out by prehistoric farmers – this wild and fascinating area is "arguably the oldest continually-worked landscape in the world".[5] Many of these fields have names that mutely testify to the churchway's passage – "Cross Close" (or "Crossclaws"), "Way Moor", "Road Croft", "Way Field", and "Cross Park". Also along the churchway are numerous granite stiles (Plate 13), some of which were used as resting spots where the coffin was prayed over and blessed, as recorded in an account of the walking funeral of a drowned seaman in 1832.

The Wicca-Zennor path is in fact the extension of a longer churchway connecting Wicca with numerous farms and communities to the east. The origin of the route seems, rather curiously, to be a rock outcrop on The Island (St Ives Head). As along the Wicca-Zennor segment, this eastern part of the route is marked by crosses and field names, including "Churchway" and "Road Field". These names, like those mentioned above, date back to the seventeenth and eighteenth centuries, but there are older ones in the Cornish tongue elsewhere along the churchway such as "Furrywidden" *(vorr an gwidn,* "the white way") and "Park and grouse" (grouse deriving from the Cornish for cross, *crowz).*

The name "Wicca" is somewhat mysterious. Nowadays the word is understood to relate to witchcraft, and it is true that the churchway passes by the neighbouring farm of Tregerthen (SW 466.391) on its way to Zennor. "Tregerthen" means "rowan tree farm": the rowan or mountain ash, rare in this district, is known in many parts of Britain as "the witch-tree" being almost everywhere credited with the power to avert witchcraft. The steep slope of

Burn Downs rising to the south of Tregerthen was where the witches of the area used to gather and was the location of Witches' Rock (broken up in the nineteenth century). Furthermore, folklore tells of a witch at Trewey, a village immediately adjacent to Zennor, who, when having her powers challenged by her husband, turned into a hare and ran to St Ives and back within thirty minutes bringing food for her doubtless chastened spouse. The route she used as described in the folktale was, effectively, the churchway. Despite all these references to witchcraft, most scholars would probably argue that Wicca derives from the Anglo-Saxon word for settlement, *hwicce*. But if this is so, why should this farm be the only one in the area not to have a Cornish name?

The Wicca-Zennor churchway is easy and delightful to walk, and as Weatherhill correctly states, it is this stretch of the path "which most strongly retains a sense of Otherworldness". Its course has been co-opted into the modern, signposted South West Coast Path leisure walk. As this is followed, it cuts down past a barn and along the churchyard wall to the lych-gate at St Senara's church in Zennor. However, this is a deviation from the course of the ancient route that continued to a cross, of which only the base now survives, some hundreds of yards west of the church. Weatherhill points out that instead of being treated as separate churchways, this whole route can be traced as a single entity passing on westward beyond Zennor through fields with churchway-related names and with crosses dotted along it, connecting a string of communities – Boswednack, Porthmeor, Bosigran, Trevowhan, to mention just some – reaching the villages of Morvah and Pendeen.

The churchway bypasses not only the church at Zennor, but also the ones at St Ives and Morvah. "If this so-called churchway was not associated with the parish churches, or, it would seem, the sites of early Christian chapels, then why the waymark crosses?" asks Weatherhill.[6] He concludes that it may initially have been a pre-Christian ceremonial route, its pagan origins perhaps being recalled in its folk associations with witchcraft. Earlier Christianity in Cornwall was of a Celtic nature, closer to pagan traditions, but later mainstream medieval Christianity may have placed its churches slightly off the direct route, due to a sense of caution or distaste regarding its early pagan connections.

An irony is that this route was followed in the eighteenth century by John Wesley, the founder of Methodism. He preached and lodged at points along it, and Methodist chapels were built directly on its path at several places. A ruined one can be found on the Wicca-Zennor churchway between Wicca and Tregerthen. There is no road or track leading to this building except for the churchway. (This route was first brought to my attention by the work of Craig Weatherhill.)

CUMBRIA
●5. ARNSIDE to BEETHAM via the "Fairy Steps"
Explorer 1:25,000 O.S. map no. OL7 ("The English Lakes [SE]"). This corpse road is situated about 5 miles (8 km) north of Carnforth. Its total length, if taken from the coastal Arnside area all the way eastward to Beetham village (on a loop road off the A6 1½ miles (2.5 km) south of Milnthorpe), is in excess of 2 miles (3.2 km).

Arnside is on the estuary of the Kent River where it issues into Morecombe Bay. The river is subject to a tidal bore, a swift and dangerous high tide that races up from the bay. In prehistoric times much of the area was underwater, and it has long been subject to inundation even in later historic times, but the Arnside district has since been drained, though there are still marshes (called "mosses" locally). Until the middle of the nineteenth century, Arnside was a small fishing village, but with the building of the railway there its population grew. A church was also built, in 1866, but before then the villagers had to take their dead to Beetham, a full 2 miles (3.2 km) to the east, by means of a corpse way which was also a route for commercial traffic. It remains well marked on the map as a leisure walk (the Limestone Link).

The corpse way effectively starts at SD 464.783 by a railway track, and proceeds as a causeway eastward across Arnside Moss and over a wooden footbridge spanning Leighton Beck. The route then crosses the motor road to Carr Bank and carries on through partially exposed limestone country to Hazelslack Tower Farm (SD 477.788), the "tower" element in the name being a reference to a fifteenth-century stone fortress whose ruins are still substantial. This was one of numerous such structures in the region designed to protect against raiders from the north. Hazelslack, the beginning of the most interesting section of the corpse way, is patrolled by its free-roaming resident peacocks, which are often to be seen standing proudly on the farmhouse roof. Hazelslack was previously known as "Helslack"; "slack" is an old term for gully or ravine, while "hel" could have been a reference to the corpse road – for instance, a corpse road in Yorkshire (entry 22) was known as the "Old Hell Way".

A signpost indicating the direction to the "Fairy Steps" stands by a stone stile a few yards from the farm. The path goes straight along the edge of fields and through a further stone wall-stile to Underlaid Wood, which it enters. This stage of the route has a truly magical feel, with the dense, mixed woodland casting everything in a soft green twilight. The path looks its ancient best here, the limestone being worn almost bare. It runs in a straight line and rises gradually in a series of shallow terraces or "bars", a result of the way the limestone was deposited long ages ago. After about half a mile (0.8 km) the path comes to Whin Scar ("scar" is the regional term for a cliff or rocky outcrop) and

Plate 14. Rock gully at Whin Scar on the course of the Arnside-to-Beetham corpse road, Cumbria.

Plate 15. The Fairy Steps.

the route ascends in two stages. The first is a set of shallow steps leading up through a rocky gully (Plate 14). This opens out onto a relatively open area where a signpost directs to "Beetham via the Fairy Steps". A hundred yards or so (100 m) further on there looms a grey cliff-face. The walker on the path ascends by means of an angled flight of very narrow and steep rock-cut steps set within a deep fissure in the cliff – these are the Fairy Steps (Plate 15). Local tradition has it that the whole area is haunted by fairies, and that they will grant a wish to anyone able to hop up the steps without touching the sides of the cleft. The task is virtually impossible because the steps are so irregular and sinuous and in places the cleft is only a foot (30 cm) wide at shoulder height, so any full-size adult climbing them has to turn at an angle to do so. Indeed, the process is like a crash course in claustrophobia. This only underlines how awkward it must have been for travellers carrying anything, whether a corpse in a coffin or a sack of flour, to get past this barrier. The problem was managed by means of a rope being passed through an iron ring set high up in the rock face close to the steps, so enabling the raising or lowering of goods.

The cliff-top allows fine views back over the top of Underlaid Wood toward the Kent estuary and the mountains of the Lake District far beyond. Onward, there is a choice of paths, but the person wishing to trace the route of the corpse road takes the one leading off more or less straight ahead. This takes a fairly direct but not consistently straight route through more woodland, finally leading down a slope to a gate at the edge of the trees overlooking Beetham village. The path follows an indistinct course across an open field to join a motor road at one end of the village.

The final destination for funeral processions using the corpse road was the church of St Michael and All Angels in Beetham (SD 496.795). Much of the present structure is a Victorian renovation of a primarily medieval church, though there are remains of Norman stonework in the fabric, and the base of the church tower is of Saxon origin, so a church has stood on the site for over a thousand years. In the nineteenth century, during early renovation work and grave-digging in the nave, the foundations of an earlier church building were uncovered along with hoards of silver coins dating back to the time of William the Conqueror and, even earlier, to Edward the Confessor and King Canute.

Today the Wheatsheaf Inn close to the church affords refreshment for corpse road travellers, but in earlier times the former Blue Bell inn virtually on the edge of the churchyard would doubtless have performed this function for the mourners. Cottages now stand on its site in Church Street. (This route was first brought to my attention by Danny Sullivan, [7] citing the work of Graham Dugdale.[8])

●6. MARDALE (HAWESWATER) to SHAP

Landranger 1:50,000 O.S. map no.90 ("Penrith & Keswick"). This is one of the very few corpse roads actually to be marked as such on the map, and runs for 7 miles (12 km) from Haweswater Reservoir to the village of Shap on the A6 close to junction 39 on the M6.

This formerly well-known corpse road used to start out from the village of Mardale Green, but that has now disappeared beneath the surface of the Haweswater Reservoir. This blends into the charming Lakeland landscape as if it had always been there, but in fact the reservoir was formed in 1937 when Mardale was flooded to accommodate it. The chapel at Mardale had been granted its own burial ground in 1728, and the last corpse from Mardale was taken along the corpse road to the mother church at Shap in 1736. So, prior to the flooding, there were bodies to be exhumed from Mardale graveyard. The remains were placed in tin boxes. As this was a sensitive issue their removal was left until the dead of night. The remains were transported by truck through the nearby village of Bampton (situated close to what is now the northerly end of the reservoir) and on to Shap for reburial. Elderly folk in Bampton still insist that bones could be heard rattling in the tin boxes as

Plate 16. The flooded site of Mardale Green, Haweswater, Cumbria. This photograph was taken when the reservoir waters were a little low, and exposed stone field walls can be discerned by the water's edge in the foreground.

the trucks tried to pass stealthily through the village.

In long spells of hot weather, when the water level is particularly low, parts of Mardale become visible and can be spied from the dead-end reservoir road out of Bampton that hugs the high slopes on the eastern edge of Haweswater (Plate 16). The corpse way now starts from this road at NY 4795.1185, a mile (1.5 km) from the parking area at the end and close to a picturesque waterfall. Next to the roadside gate where the rough track leads up onto the moorland of Mardale Common there is a weathered signpost that actually indicates that it is the "Old Corpse Way" (see back jacket).

The course of the corpse road crosses Mardale Common and then zigzags its way down the steep far side into the isolated little valley of Swindale. It becomes a broad, if heavily-rutted, way between drystone walling as it descends to the small farm of Swindale Head at NY 505.125 (Plate 17). From here the corpse road used to follow the valley floor alongside the river, Swindale Beck, via an eighteenth-century chapel of ease, [9] but now the permissible route is along the narrow lane leading down the valley from Swindale Head to Truss Gap (NY 515.132). There, Swindale Beck can be crossed by stepping stones or a more recent footbridge. The trackway becomes clearly visible a short distance on beyond the river, where it begins its long, angled ascent up the steep slopes of Ralfland Forest, the last stretch of bleak, exposed moorland before Shap. Although funerary usage of the road from

Plate 17. The Mardale-to-Shap corpse road descending to Swindale Head, its rutted course marked by stone walls on either side.

Mardale supposedly ceased in the eighteenth century, it is reportedly the case that at least some of Swindale's dead continued to be taken to Shap by this route until 1939.

The section of the route over Ralfland Forest and into Shap is known as the Kirk Gate – vernacular for "Church Road". Its course across the wilderness is largely ill-defined, but it becomes a clearly visible low causeway (Plate 18) as it passes close to the lonely farmstead of Tailbert (NY 533.145), the site of an old Norse settlement. Here, the track transforms into an unfenced metalled moorland lane that leads gradually down toward Shap. On its way, it passes immediately by Keld Chapel (NY 564.154), a plain, medieval structure now in the care

Plate 18. The Mardale-to-Shap corpse road appearing as a slightly raised track near the moorland farmstead of Tailbert.

of the National Trust. This was doubtless a coffin resting place before the chapel was built, and may possibly have acted as a chapel of ease when the corpse road was still in use. The metalled road deviates from the course of the old corpse way as it approaches Shap; that course is preserved as a footpath that leaves the road at a sharp corner at NY 5581.1410 and passes by a massive prehistoric monolith known as the Goggleby Stone (Plate 19) situated at NY 5590.1510. This is the survivor of a megalithic avenue, a way of the

Plate 19. The Goggleby Stone, near Shap.

dead far older than the one we have been tracing here. (It is curious to note how here, as elsewhere, some medieval corpse ways seem to echo prehistoric routes and pass by Stone Age features.) In Shap, the course of the footpath is taken over by a road in the built-up area that aligns toward journey's end – the church of St Michael. This was restored in the nineteenth century but may have origins older than the medieval Shap Abbey near the village.

Although this corpse road weaves around to accommodate steep slopes, and by doing so obviously adds many miles to the as-the-crow-flies distance of 7 miles (11 km), its fundamental course is surprisingly direct – key points along it, such as the starting point, Truss Gate, and the Goggleby Stone and church at Shap, all fall on a straight line. As a local informant put it, "... it is more or less a direct line from Mardale reet to Shap church".[10] (This corpse road was first brought to my attention by the late Jim Taylor Page.)

●7. RYDAL to GRASMERE

Explorer 1:25,000 O.S. map no. OL7 ("The English Lakes [SE]"). Rydal lies about 5 road miles (8 km) south-east of Grasmere, and is situated just off the main A591 motor road. Depending on the number of visitors, there is usually parking along the short road leading up to Rydal Mount from the main road.

This corpse road, starting at Rydal and ending in Grasmere in the heart of the Lake District, offers a delightful walk through a glorious landscape. It is a spirit road in every sense, in that it raises the spirits of the living and would have been a fitting final journey for the dead. More than that, something of the

Plate 20. Looking along the Rydale-to-Grasmere corpse road, Cumbria.

spirit of the landscape it traverses lives on in the work of the great nature poet, William Wordsworth, with whom this path is closely associated.

The public footpath that now preserves the course of the old corpse way and church path must be followed from the Rydal end if it is to trace the route taken by the funeral processions and churchgoers of old. Rydal (NY 3645.0640) is a tiny cluster of buildings incorporating Rydal Hall and grounds, the church, and Rydal Mount, the home of the Wordsworth family from 1813 until William's death in 1850, and that of his wife, Mary, in 1859. Rydal did not have a church until 1824, when the chapel of St Mary was built by Lady le Fleming of Rydal Hall. Wordsworth wrote about the founding of the church, for which he helped to select the site. Because it was located on rocky ground, no burials were performed there.

The path starts at a gate up behind Rydal Mount and takes a gently undulating course along the valley side, beneath Nab Scar (Plate 20). For the first part of its length there are stunning views of Rydal Water, far below. This is a small but beautiful lake, and one of the first to freeze in winter, when it becomes a popular venue for skating – a pleasure undertaken there by Wordsworth. The Wordsworths are buried in the churchyard in Grasmere, and it would be interesting to know if their funerals were processed along this track, though possibly by the 1850s such usage had fallen into decline. However, it is known that Wordsworth often walked this route between Rydal and Grasmere, its directness between the two places making its 2-mile (3-km) length shorter than the journey by the winding main road in the valley below. About a mile (1.5 km) along the track from Rydal, a substantial block of stone is encountered on the right-hand side. This is known locally as the Resting or Coffin Stone (Plate 21). It is a two-tier feature consisting of the main rock for resting the coffin on with a seat built against it for the bearers. The path continues on toward Grasmere, eventually becoming a metalled minor road that leads down past Dove Cottage, another famous Wordsworth dwelling, where he wrote much of his poetry. Formerly an inn called the Dove and Olive, the poet came to live at the cottage in 1799 along with his sister, Dorothy, famed for her journals. Mary moved in with them in 1802 after her marriage to William, and they had three of their five children there. In addition to Thomas De Quincey, who lodged with them, there were many famous literary visitors to Dove Cottage, including Walter Scott, Charles and Mary Lamb, Robert Southey, and the Wordsworths' great friend, Samuel Taylor Coleridge. It became too cramped for them to continue living at the cottage, so they moved out in 1808. After relatively short stays elsewhere, they finally settled at Rydal Mount.

The course of the corpse way continues past Dove Cottage and crosses the A591 main road, finally following the B5287 into Grasmere where it becomes the village's high street, leading directly to St Oswald's church, which stands on the site of an earlier, twelfth-century, church.

There is no better antidote to world-weariness than a walk along this ancient way between Rydal and Grasmere, to follow where Wordsworth walked, and, perhaps with a few of his works to hand, to feel the poet's spirit alongside. (This corpse way was first brought to my attention by the late Jim Taylor Page.)

Plate 21. The Coffin Stone on the Rydale-to-Grasmere corpse road.

Plate 22. The hilltop crossroads at Down St Mary, Devon. The former schoolhouse is the building behind the white Land Rover. The top of the church tower is visible above the trees beyond.

DEVON
●8. DOWN ST MARY

Landranger 1:50,000 O.S. map, no.191 ("Okehampton & North Dartmoor – Crediton & Bovey Tracey"). The village of Down St Mary is situated on minor roads a short distance to the south-west of the A377, 7 miles (11 km) to the north-west of Crediton.

There is a long-standing piece of folklore in this small hilltop village claiming that on certain nights a ghostly black dog with glowing eyes runs down the main street, striking a projecting corner of the former schoolhouse as it passes by (Plate 22). It is a wholly phantom event, however, because though masonry is apparently heard to fall no visible damage occurs. The former schoolhouse building stands very close to the church (SS 743.045), which has a notable Norman (or earlier) tympanum over its south door (Plate 23). This shows a dog-like creature, and it is open to speculation as to whether this relates to the ghostly black dog legend. If so, it goes back at least a whole millennium.

The old schoolhouse building stands at a hilltop crossroads, and it is probable that not only the high street but other roads coming in here were used as churchways and thus corpse roads. Access to the church was past the building, and so this legend may connect with the idea of the black dog as barguest, the "spirit of the bier" (see Chapter Three).

Barbara Carbonell was an early twentieth-century follower of Alfred Watkins' ley (alignments of sites) theory, and she lived in this area of north Devon. She found several black dog legends in the district, and, further,

Plate 23. The ancient tympanum in the church at Down St Mary. The dog-like creature is on the right.

plotted about a dozen of them occurring in roughly a straight line from Copplestone Cross, 2 miles (3.2 km) south-east of Down St Mary, through to Great Torrington, 20 miles (32 km) to the north-west. Down St Mary was just one example on this overall route.

●9. THE LYCH WAY: BELLEVER to LYDFORD, Dartmoor National Park Explorer 1:25,000 O.S. map no.OL28, ("Dartmoor"). The approximately 12-mile (19 km) Lych Way starts at Bellever, accessed by a well-marked forestry track leading off the B3212 road immediately after an area of woodland surrounding Bellever Tor and just before the village of Postbridge (where there is an excellent National Park Centre selling guidebooks, maps, compasses, and other useful items, and where wardens are on hand to give advice, for example on routes and weather conditions; there are also parking facilities and toilets). There are parking areas in the wood. At the other end of the route, Lydford is situated at the north-west corner of Dartmoor, just off the A386, 7 miles (11 km) north of Tavistock.

The Lych Way is Dartmoor's Road of the Dead, one of the more celebrated of England's corpse ways. Despite this it is a road less travelled today, for even some of the ramblers who use the recreational public footpath it has now become do not understand that they are on an old corpse way, and know little about such features.

"Lych", of course, comes from liches, Old English for corpse. The relatively small number of early medieval dwellers of central Dartmoor were obliged to carry their dead to Lydford Church, situated on the north-west rim of the moor, because this was, and still is, the parish church for Dartmoor, giving it one of the largest parishes in England. Furthermore, the Lych Way was not only a corpse road but also a general churchway, which had to be used whenever sacramental purposes demanded. It was a gruelling journey, some 12 miles (19 km) long in the best of times, and in bad weather its length could be extended by 5-6 miles (8-10 km) when diversions had to be taken to avoid swollen rivers and dangerously boggy ground. In 1260, inhabitants of the most easterly moorland homesteads, or "tenements" as they were called, successfully petitioned the Bishop of Exeter, Walter Bronescombe, for dispensation to attend the much nearer Widecombe church (see the next entry). But as the most direct route to Lydford, which remained the hub for religious and administrative matters associated with Dartmoor, the track continued to be used for both spiritual and secular traffic until the early nineteenth century.

The beginning of the Lych Way is taken by common agreement to be the medieval clapper bridge over the East Dart River at Bellever (SX 6583.7732). Many ancient tracks led to the hamlet of Believer (the former Bellaford), and funeral parties bringing their dead from further east on the moor would have passed it by. A ford preceded the clapper bridge, and a nineteenth-century arched bridge now stands alongside its remnants (Plate 24). From the bridge the modern metalled forestry road alongside the trees approximates the original course of the Lych Way for some of its distance. The Lych Way now heads off north-west across the moor from the B3212 road at SX 6375.7766; this is a recent re-routing, the original route crossing the road a little further

Plate 24. Remnants of the old clapper bridge at Bellever, Dartmoor, start of the Lych Way. The arched nineteenth-century bridge is next to it.

Plate 25. Wistman's Wood, lair of the spectral Wish Hounds of Dartmoor, and adjacent to the course of the Lych Way.

south along the B3212 where Cherry Brook crosses, but this apparently became increasingly difficult to navigate owing to marshy conditions. Either route can be shown on Ordnance Survey maps, depending on the date of the edition referred to.

The Lych Way proper is resumed after a short distance beyond Powder Mills Farm, where gunpowder was manufactured in the nineteenth century. This is reportedly a haunted spot: the Devon folklorist, Theo Brown, recorded a 1924 eyewitness account here of a phantom "hairy hand", a relatively frequently reported ghostly sighting on Dartmoor during the early twentieth century. The witness was with her family in a caravan among the ruins of the old Powder Mill; one night she awoke to see the ghostly hand clawing its way up an end window of the caravan. She had a sense of evil, and made a sign of the cross, after which the hand sank out of sight.[11] The corpse road continues in an increasingly ill-defined way up and over open moorland past Longaford Tor and then descends down toward the West Dart river, passing just to the north of Wistman's Wood (SX 612.774). This is an ancient grove of gnarled, lichen-encrusted and stunted oak trees that have grown into fantastic, contorted shapes amid the litter of grey granite boulders that in ages past rolled down from Littaford Tors above into the valley (Plate 25). An important haven for wildlife, this woodland has long been a Nature Conservancy reserve. Perhaps because of the weird shapes of the trees, the isolation of the grove, the proximity of the Lych Way, or all these factors combined, Wistman's Wood also has a reputation for being a haunted place. The prime association is with the "Wish Hounds", the phantom pack that roams the moor at night accompanying a frightening huntsman who is perhaps the Norse god Odin or even "Dewer", the Devil himself, seeking lost souls. At dusk, the spectral hounds are said to start out on their grim forays from Wistman's Wood, issuing chilling howls. There is a Dartmoor folktale that tells of a farmer riding home across the moor after a lively evening of drinking with friends. He suddenly encountered the ghostly pack and its dread attendant. Being still fairly drunk the farmer was unfazed, and he yelled out that he hoped they had enjoyed good hunting; with a laugh the Devil responded by saying he would make the man a gift of the kill, and threw him a bundle. The man continued his homeward ride, not opening the gift until he dismounted outside his door. When he unwrapped it he found that instead of the expected haunch of venison he had instead been carrying a dead baby – his own.

The legend of the Wish Hounds is a version of the very ancient Europe-wide belief in the Wild Hunt, which howled through the night sky led by some pagan god or goddess, or another mythical personage, gathering up the souls of the those who had just died, or who happened to be in its path, and taking them off to the Otherworld.[12] Dartmoor as a whole has a particularly rich collection of phantom hound legends, and it was one of these that inspired Conan Doyle's Sherlock Holmes mystery, *The Hound of the Baskervilles*. The curious "Wish" name for the uncanny canines of Wistman's Wood has caused some debate. The most common explanation is that it derives from "wisht" a West-country term for spooky, itself coming from "Wise", a regional name for Odin.[13] Ruth St Leger-Gordon has written that "Wistman" could similarly belong to the same source. "Small wonder then that Wistman's Wood, the Lych Path above it, and the scattered remains of a prehistoric village nearby are reputedly haunted, " she remarked.[14] There have also been claimed eyewitness reports of apparitions in the vicinity of the wood. In one case, visitors reported seeing a phantom funeral procession of white-robed monks emerge from one end of the wood and head toward the river below, where they faded away.

The Lych Way comes to a wooden gate and small stile in a fence close to the river half a mile (0.8 km) north of Wistman's Wood, and in good weather the river is easily crossed here. The route continues, still in an undefined manner, diagonally up the slope beyond, passing closely to the left of Lydford Tor, which becomes visible after cresting the slope. (Unless one wishes to risk continuing along the Lych Way in spirit form, it is important to note that here the route enters the perimeter of an army firing range, marked by a range notice board,

Plate 26. Travellers' Ford, on the Lych Way in the heart of Dartmoor – site of an apparent paranormal incident.

so it is important to check at the National Park Centre in Postbridge whether the range is in use before setting out to walk the Lych Way.) The route bears gently to the right – northward – descending all the time from the rocky outcrop of the tor, coming to a farm gate in a stone wall in just under half a mile (0.8 km). Although the Lych Way is poorly defined or, at best, a stranded route in open moorland, its true course becomes obvious at set points, such as fords, along the route. That is the case here, for shortly after the gate the Lych Way becomes a well-worn, "hollow" track that descends steeply to picturesque Travellers' Ford (SX 5915.7860) on the upper reaches of the Cowsic stream (Plate 26).

That great chronicler of Dartmoor tracks, Eric Hemery, recorded an incident at this remote place that clearly deeply affected him. It is the more striking precisely because Hemery is normally such a pragmatic writer. One day he rested by the ford sitting alongside a man who turned out to be a German visitor, completely unfamiliar with Dartmoor. "I was astonished to hear him say that many, many people had passed this place in former times, burdened with great sorrow, " Hemery recalled. "This instant revelation of the true purpose of the Lych Way was, I realized from his demeanour, the result not of telepathy between us but of genuine ESP [Extra-Sensory Perception]."[15] This unavoidably brings to mind the old practice of corpse road seership conducted by the "Precursors" of Holland and their counterparts elsewhere, discussed in Chapter Two.

The track continues on across Conies Down, and only those keen on rambling should contemplate proceeding further. The Lych Way bypasses the highest, if otherwise poor, example of a stone row on Dartmoor on the right (at SX 5858.7900) and through a ford on Prison Leat. At a point below Cocks Hill the track forks (at SX 5656.7936) and the Lych Way is the right-hand branch. It passes on alongside walling, across a ford, and drops down to the plain of Bagga Tor – the track in some parts is deeply rutted. It passes through gates and goes by Brousentor Farm (SX 5451.8067). Descent from here is via a rough lane, and past the surfaced road leading to Standon Farm on the right. The route proceeds downward to the River Tavy, keeping to the left (south) of Baggator Brook, over a stile and through a gate to the riverside, becoming ever more verdantly atmospheric and magical. Woodland to the left of the route in the latter part of this descent is Coffin Wood, which extends down to the river a short distance further south. When mourners were taking a corpse along the Lych Way it would have been carried on the back of a pack-horse, probably in a special canvas sack, with the bearers walking alongside. At Coffin Wood, however, the body would have been transferred to a coffin for the remainder of the journey to Lydford. The procedure seems to have been that someone would go ahead of the funeral procession and forewarn specialist pall-bearers at Coffin Wood of its approach. These would then meet the party with an empty coffin, the transaction would be undertaken, and the corpse in its coffin borne across the river.

At the River Tavy the walker is faced with the stepping-stone crossing known as the Cataloo Steps (Plate 27) alongside the point where Baggator Brook flows into the river (SX 5400.8112). In dry spells, when the water is low and the river tame, it is easy to cross the river here using the large stones. But in wet weather this can be a dangerous place, with substantial volumes of water coursing through. So caution must be exercised, depending on conditions. There is a footbridge over the adjoining Baggator Brook leading to a path that goes to the Standon Steps, a short distance further north, where the Tavy can be crossed by a footbridge. This is

Plate 27. The "Cataloo Steps", the old crossing point of the Lych Way on the River Tavy, photographed on a calm summer's morning.

the route used by most people today, but it is the Cataloo crossing that preserves the old course of the Lych Way.

On the other side of the Tavy an ancient green road leads up from the stepping stones. This is Corpse Lane (Plate 28). At the top end of this rarely used sunken way, where it fades away into the landscape, the walker has to use the map and what signing there is to trace the route through gates and stiles and across a field to a lane that leads up to Higher Willsworthy Farm (SX 5359.8167). Here the route joins a surfaced country lane. Using the 1:25, 000-scale map, the route can be traced for another 2 miles (3 km) from here into Lydford, but it was not explored during the fieldwork for this Sampler.

Part of the course of the corpse road is marked by Silver Street in the ancient village of Lydford. The church, dedicated to St Petroc, was built in the thirteenth century, but there was an earlier, timber church at Lydford in Saxon times.

This route, explored whole or in part, is not to be undertaken lightly and without some planning, especially by those not used to long-distance hiking. Weather conditions and firing times on the military range should be checked before setting off; a 1:25,000-scale map is essential, and a compass is advised. Carry water, if not food, and, in case of some dire emergency, it would be wise to take a (switched off) mobile phone. For more experienced walkers who want to savour the full eeriness of the Lych Way, there is an organised night walk held along it every October. It starts from a pub in Lydford or Widecombe, on alternate years, and is led by an experienced guide.[16]

Plate 28. The ancient Corpse Lane on the course of the Lych Way, leading up from the River Tavy.

● 10. MERRIVALE STONE ROWS, Dartmoor

Explorer 1:25,000 O.S. map. No.OL28 ("Dartmoor"). The Bronze Age stone rows are a few hundred yards south of the B3357 road between Tavistock and Two Bridges. They can be accessed on foot from the car pull-in on the south side of the road less than 1 mile (1.5 km) past the Merrivale quarry (on the other, north, side of the road).

The Merrivale rows are probably the most accessible good examples of the site type. They are two double rows running parallel with one another on a roughly east-west alignment at SX 553.746. The northern double row is about 600 ft (180 m) long; the southern row runs for nearly 900 ft (270 m). Both sets of rows have triangular "blocking stones" at their eastern ends, and one double row has two pillar-shaped blocking stones at the other end. Near the centre of the southern row, there is a round burial mound or barrow surrounded by a circle of stones. A barrow to the south-west of the twin set of double rows also has the remains of a stone row leading out from it to the south-west.

Taken as a whole, this site complex provides the opportunity to consider the argument put forward in Chapter Five that the rows represent spirit ways for the souls of the persons who were buried in the mounds. A short walk to the south of this complex of rows there is a circle of low stones and a tall monolith.

● 11. PIZWELL to WIDECOMBE-on-the-MOOR

Explorer 1:25,000 O.S. map no.OL28 ("Dartmoor"). Access to Pizwell is via a single-track lane at Runnage Bridge on the country road to Widecombe, which runs south-east from the B3212 immediately after Postbridge.

After the Church's special dispensation of 1260, the people of Pizwell and some other Dartmoor homesteads or "Ancient Tenements" were able to use the church in the moorland village of Widecombe instead of Lydford. The east-to-west route they took became known as the Churchway, and is referred to as such in a document of 1491.[17] Tracks from other homesteads joined the route at various places. From Pizwell to Widecombe the route is about 4 miles (6.5 km) long, and the modern wayfarer can approximate some of its course by car.

The cluster of medieval grey buildings that is Pizwell (SX 6686.7844) is barely half a mile (0.8 km) down a narrow metalled lane leading from the small bridge at Runnage (SX 6682.7889) on the minor motor road from Postbridge. Alongside Pizwell Green runs the Walla Brook, and the ford there has changed little over the centuries (Plate 29). As it started out on its solemn journey, the funeral party would have crossed this and proceeded along the path that extends westward from it. After half a mile (0.8 km) this track joins the motor road (at SX 6776.7852) opposite woodland (Soussons Warren). From this point the road approximates the old Churchway for a few miles, passing on the right Grendon

Cottage and the entrance road to Grendon Farm, Lower Blackaton and, at a sharp bend, the entrance drive to Blackaton Manor, and the cottage of Gamble Cot, just prior to a T-junction marked on the upright of the signpost there as Blackaton (SX 698.778). One arm of the signpost indicates Challacombe, and the Challacombe branch of the Churchway joined at this junction. The route continues – now as a track – through a gate and up the slope of the hillside facing the road junction. The trackway crosses the ridge in a south-easterly direction, and

Plate 29. On the Pizwell-to-Widecombe churchway, Dartmoor, looking back at the hamlet of Pizwell across the Walla Brook stepping stones.

intersects the Two Moors Way on the summit plateau before commencing a well-defined descent, with enclosed land on the left and the great tower of St Pancras church in Widecombe visible ahead and far below. A gate allows exit off the open moor, and a trackway continues the descent beyond. This becomes a tarmac lane that descends with increasing steepness into Widecombe.

The church tower dates from *c.*1500, but the origins of the rest of the building dates from the fourteenth century. Set within the expansive village green, it is so large and impressive that it has often been referred to as "the cathedral of the moors". In 1638, during a severe thunderstorm, lightning struck a pinnacle of the tower and it crashed through the roof; contemporary reports tell of a great fiery ball that rolled through the church. Four people were killed instantly and another 62 were injured, some of them dying later. Anomalies were reported: one man was burnt to death yet his clothes were hardly singed, another survived but found his money melted inside his otherwise undamaged wallet. Others found their underclothes scorched while their outer garments were untouched. Rumours subsequently abounded that the Devil had been out and about.

The moorland village's most famous association, though, is undoubtedly the folksong, "Widdecombe Fair", collected in a village just north of Dartmoor by the famous Devonshire vicar and author, Sabine Baring-Gould, in the nineteenth century:

Tom Pearse, Tom Pearse, lend me your grey mare,
All along, down along, out along lee,
For I want for to go to Widdecombe Fair,
Wi' Bill Brewer, Jan Stewer, Peter Gurney,
Peter Davey, Dan I Whiddon, Harry Hawk,
Old Uncle Tom Cobley and all,
Old Uncle Tom Cobley and all!

And so on for several verses more. The basic storyline is that the motley crew do not return with the grey mare when expected, so Tom Pearse goes looking for it. He finds the creature on top of a hill – and he knows she is his mare because she has only one foot shod. She is in such a sorry state that she is making out her will! It is implied that her eight (probably drunken) riders proved too much for her, and that they all came to an untimely end. The mare, too, takes sick and dies, causing Tom Pearse to sit down on a rock and cry. The animal is buried,

But this isn't the end o' this shocking affair,
All along, down along, out along lee,
Nor, though they be dead, of the horrid career,
Of Bill Brewer, Jan Stewer, etc.

When the wind whistles cold on the moor of a night,
All along, down along, out along lee,
Tom Pearse s old mare doth appear gashley white,
Wi' Bill Brewer, Jan Stewer, etc.

And all the night long be heard skirling and groans,
All along, down along, out along lee,
From Tom Pearse's old mare in her rattling bones,
And from Bill Brewer, Jan Stewer, etc.

There are various versions of the song, and the names of most of the mare's riders vary in every locality; their identity is unknown though their surnames do occur in the localities in question. However, Tom Cobley is known to have been a real person: he was a prosperous farmer who lived in the Devon village of Spreyton. Tom Pearse (or Pearce) appears in every version of the song, and though his identity has not been authoritatively confirmed there was a mill-owner by that name in the village of Sticklepath and some argue that he was the fellow in question.[18] But Theo Brown found versions of the song as widely separated geographically as Cornwall and Northumbria, and Tom Pearse still appears, so it seems the name had some generalized association. "It was plainly a song that belonged nowhere but lent itself freely to local adaptation, " she observed.[19] The identity of the eighth person, the singer, the one asking Tom Pearse for his grey mare, is not given in the song.

In a brilliant piece of scholarship, [20] unfortunately too complex to properly enter into here, Brown traced the basic motif of the song to Continental influence, for tin miners came to Britain from mainland Europe during Elizabethan times, and Dartmoor, like Cornwall and other areas of the British Isles, was important for its tin mines. (Indeed, it was the wealth of the local Guild of Tinners that enabled such an impressive church to be built at Widecombe.) Some of the European miners were German, many coming from the Harz mountains, a region that relinquished its pagan traditions with reluctance and provided many of the motifs in the fairytales of the Grimm brothers. A ghostly image in German lore is *der Schimmelreiter,* the Rider on the White Horse. *Schimmel* actually denotes a grey or mildew colour, and the English word "shimmer" meaning a tremulous or subdued light derives from it. An earlier meaning, though, was to "shine brightly". "This mixture of meanings may explain why we speak of 'Windsor Greys', which of course are snowy white, " Brown commented. In a work appearing long after Theo Brown's research, C P Biggam made a specific study of "grey" in Old English and similarly found that linguistic elements relating to the term had a much less specific colour meaning than is the case in the modern language, and often denoted a grey/white tone plus numerous non-colour associations such as fearsome, sinister, and boundary as well as more obvious ones such as age.[21]

Brown traced other associations with mares and greyness that originated in Continental Europe, perhaps as far back as the pagan Celtic Iron Age. One set of examples involves the Welsh Mari Lwyd, the Irish Lair Bhan, and Laare Vane from the Isle of Man. All these names mean white or grey mare. In the Marie Lwyd New Year tradition, which has been revived in recent years after a moribund period, a horse's skull on a pole is paraded around. Such traditions hark back to the sanctity of the horse in Iron Age Celtic beliefs, its most extreme form occurring as ritual bestiality in pagan Celtic kingship rites. The Roman goddess-mare, Epona, echoes similar associations, and the Celtic Rhiannon likewise. In a story from the *Mabinogion,* Arawn, king of Annwn, the underworld, is mounted on a light grey steed. Brown failed to mention that the Norse shaman-god Odin rode an eight-legged mare called Sleipnir, but she did suggest that the ultimate source of the associations could perhaps be traced back across the steppes to Central Asian shamanism, in which the horse was thought of as a psychopomp, a guide to the Otherworld. The Altai shaman, for instance, had a grey or light-coloured horse killed so that its spirit could act as his steed to take him on his magical, entranced journey to the spirit realms. Brown concluded that Pearse's grey mare represents "an indeterminate entity hovering between night and day, or between life and death: indeed a boundary figure". It was the supernatural steed that took people into the Otherworld, but in this "shocking affair" the death-mare died herself. "Tom Pearce therefore sits down and cries, and the dead are condemned for ever to wander homeless, unable to pass to the Otherworld, just as in classical and other beliefs ghosts cannot enter the destined world where their ancestors await them until the funeral rites have been performed in due order, " Brown opined. And the song gives the clue as to why the grey mare died – she was improperly shod. The image of the spectral skeletons of Uncle Tom Cobbley and all rattling around the moor on their equally skeletal steed may have a parallel in the Dartmoor legend of Old Crockern, said to ride a skeletal horse near Crockern Tor on stormy nights.

Brown went on to make some intriguing observations concerning the name of Widecombe itself. Versions of the name (Baring-Gould's spelling was just one) are quite common in Devon, and it means "Willow Valley", but a place-name researcher in the nineteenth century asking about the meaning of the Widecombe name was answered by someone quoting a children's riddle in local dialect:

Widdicote, Woddicote, over-cote hang;
Nothing so broad and nothing so lang
As Widdicote, Woddicote, over-cote hang.

This was a reference to the sky. Brown noted another children's saying in Devon to the effect that when it snowed it was because "Widecombe folk are plucking their geese", a reference to the down-like appearance of snowflakes. In Cornwall, though, a similar saying had the Old Sky Woman plucking the big Sky Goose that lived in the Sky Meadows beyond the clouds. "So it looks as though Widecombe is meaningful simply because it resembles an old dialect word for the Otherworld in the sky, " Brown reasoned. The linkage of the death-mare with the sky conjures up associations with the Wild Hunt, a factor that Brown herself acknowledged. The Old Crockern story further echoes this.

The "Widdecombe Fair" song, then, seems to have been a darkly humorous invention based on some very old associations to do with transit to the

Otherworld, which the name of Widecombe itself symbolized due to a phonetic coincidence that would surely not have been lost on those from far and wide across the moor, from Pizwell, Runnage, Challacombe, Babeny and other homesteads, who used the Churchway to carry their dead to burial in the village.

Plate 30. The Plush-to-Buckland corpse road, Dorset, leading up toward Ball Hill from The Folly.

DORSET
● 12. PLUSH to BUCKLAND NEWTON
1:50,000 First Series O.S. map no.194 ("Dorchester & Weymouth"). Plush is reached via a minor road off to the east of the B3143 at Piddletrenthide, about 10 miles (16 km) north-north-east of Dorchester. The village of Buckland Newton further north is less than ½ mile (0.8 km) off to the west of the B3143.

The hamlet of Plush (SY 714.021) is truly off the beaten track among the leafy old lanes of Dorset. It was made a dependent chapelry of Buckland Newton, nearly 5 miles (8 km) to the north-west, in Saxon times. The former site of an ancient chapel at Plush is marked on the 1:25,000 map, and a more recent one still stands by the road that passes through the hamlet. Coffins were carried along this road up to the crossroads at the Folly (ST 728.032), where the cortege turned left to go up over first Ball Hill, then Church Hill (Plate 30).

A signposted bridleway follows most of the course of the old corpse road. Along the ridge of Church Hill the path's route falls between two areas of woodland: it is along this stretch that local lore claims the ghostly sounds of a bier cart can be heard. The route descends the open brow of Church Hill,

Plate 31. The narrow course of the Plush-
to-Buckland corpse road where it leads
down off Church Hill towards Henley.

Plate 32. Death's door: the portal at Holy
Rood church, Buckland Newton, through
which the coffin was traditionally taken.

and becomes a now little-used narrow way (Plate 31) as it leads steeply down to the motor road that runs through Henley, a hamlet midway between Plush and Buckland Newton. As the motor road zigzags, short stretches of marked footpath here and there through the fields straighten out the bends, revealing what had once been a more direct route for the dead on their journey to Holy Rood church at Buckland (ST 688.052). It was at this church that George Cairns, a ghost-seer from nearby Lyon's Gate, held a watch "all midsummer's night to see the spirits".[22]

Arriving at the church, the coffin was admitted by a special door on the north side of the building (Plate 32). Local tradition has it that it was from this very "death's door" that the vicar left when setting off on his journey to perform church service at Plush, walking the route of the corpse way in reverse. The villagers say that one vicar died of a heart attack on a winter's day when trying to walk the path through thick snow. This is probably an actual folk memory, because while the Plush-Buckland Newton corpse way provides a delightful walk on a summer's day, with impressive views of the Dorset landscape available from the top of Church Hill, it would have been a cruel journey in bad weather. Perhaps the last thing the poor man heard were the creaking harnesses of the horses pulling the ghostly coffin cart toward him...

On a lighter note, the traveller on this road-less-travelled can find refreshment and sustenance at either end of the journey, at the locally famous Brace of Pheasants pub in Plush, or the fine Gaggle of Geese pub in Buckland Newton. (I was first alerted to this route by the work of Jeremy Harte.[23])

GLOUCESTERSHIRE
●13. SAINTBURY
Outdoor Leisure 1:25,000 O.S. map no.45 ("The Cotswolds"). The hamlet of Saintbury is below the northwestern edge of the Cotswold hills 1½ miles (2.5 km) north-east of the village of Broadway, which is situated on the A44. The general area is 6 miles (10 km) south-east of Evesham.

This corpse road was first publicized as a "leyline" in 1979;[24] it was only years later, when the whole subject area of leys came under more critical study, did its true nature become appreciated.

The corpse road comes in as a walled pathway from the north of Saintbury and becomes a hard-surfaced trackway alongside farm buildings where it meets the B4632 road (which passes through Broadway and Willersey to the west and Weston-sub-Edge to the east). At this point there is a cross (SP 1168.4026) that was a resting point for funeral processions (Plate 33). It has a fifteenth-century shaft surmounted by a more recent Maltese cross and sundial, the original cross head having been destroyed. Across this junction with the B4632, the corpse road continues south on a metalled minor road leading up to Saintbury church (SP 1172.3944), which is dedicated to St Nicholas. The present structure is mainly Norman, but it contains fragments of an earlier, Saxon, church on the site, including a Saxon sundial on the south side of the building. There are fascinating features inside the church as well, such as an octagonal stone that has been called "the pre Christian altar" by those who suspect it pre-dates even the Saxon church, and in a wall niche there is a crude stone effigy or "doll" said to be a fertility goddess or *shiela-na-gig*. Such items hint that pagan traditions were slow to fade away in the locality.

There are excusable reasons why this corpse road was first identified as a "leyline": its line, notionally extended southward beyond the church, grazes a Bronze Age burial mound on the summit of Willersey Hill, passes through a Neolithic long barrow (SP 1178.3827) in what is now a golf course just over half a mile (0.8 km) further on, and terminates at Seven Wells (SP 1194.3464) some

Plate 33. Looking south on the Saintbury corpse road, past the fifteenth-century cross at the junction with the B4632 road near Weston-sub-Edge and on toward Saintbury church – the top of its spire is just visible above the trees in the distance.

2 miles (3.2 km) beyond that (Figure 12). Now a farm, Seven Wells was associated with witch gatherings in the Early Modern period, if not earlier, and the site not only has wells but is distinctively semi-circular in shape – which could hint that it had originally been a prehistoric feature such as a henge. All this could, of course, be coincidence, but an independent statistical analysis of the line from the crossroads to the long barrow indicated that it was likely to be beyond chance (Plate 34).[25] Part of the answer might lie in the fact that Saintbury

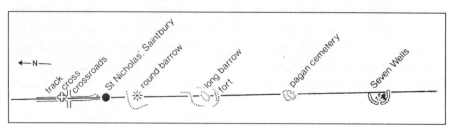

Fig. 12. Schematic plan of the "Saintbury ley". (After Ian Thomson)

Plate 34. The Saintbury corpse road as a "leyline": in this airview, the white line marks the course of the corpse road coming in from the bottom of the photograph (north), and on through the cross and crossroads pictured in Plate 33, then Saintbury church, and then the Bronze Age round barrow beyond.

lies on a Roman road known as Buckle Street, an extension of Ryknild Street further south. The map shows Buckle Street turning east at Willersey Hill and then taking a course northward past Weston-sub-Edge, but the corpse road described here parallels that course, and could have been an arm of Buckle Street if it divided at Saintbury. Either that, or the corpse road relates to the course of a prehistoric track that was re-used in part by the Romans.

LEICESTERSHIRE
●14. THURMASTON

Landranger 1:50,000 O.S. map, no.140 ("Leicester & Coventry"). The village of Thurmaston lies about 3 miles (5 km) north of Leicester city centre. It is bypassed by what is at this point the more major through route of the A607, while the high street of the old village is the A46. This is just one example of what is for non-locals the confused road situation to be found in Leicester and its immediate surroundings.

Most of the entries in this Sampler describe routes that are in areas of natural beauty, largely because the old corpse roads and churchway paths have survived best in such wild or rural areas. This example, by contrast, is in a heavily urbanized and not very pretty place, and little of the churchway survives. It is included simply because Thurmaston was my home village and as I often (and unknowingly) used the churchway as a child I can give an eyewitness account of what has now disappeared. In addition, I had a most remarkable experience one time while walking along it.

Thurmaston was originally two ancient settlements, but the modern village that developed from them is now stretched roughly north-south along the Roman Fosseway, which forms the high street. There were once two churches, the former St John's chapel for the northern part of the community and St Michael and All Angels church for the southern part. This latter became the parish church when the parishes became united in 1841. It stands (at SP 610.094) alongside the high street. Parts of the nave date from 1220, and the tower was built in the fifteenth century. The southern end of the churchway is marked by Church Lane, which runs straight alongside the churchyard wall.

Although not evident to the casual observer standing on Thurmaston high street, a modest hill rises gradually behind the church – known, reasonably enough, as Church Hill. Until a few decades ago the churchway descended the open slope of this hill from its crest across what was known as Church Field, until enclosure in the eighteenth century, and connected with a stile by the churchyard at the head of Church Lane. It was a "hollow way", a deeply worn old dirt track, known locally as the Pingle; as one walked down its straight course the church was clearly visible ahead. The track is documented on the first (1860) edition of the Ordnance Survey map of the district , but it has vanished on the ground. At the top end of Church Lane, by the church, all that is now to be found is the entrance to a footpath that goes off at right-angles; the old stile has been replaced by a high garden fence, and the churchway that existed beyond it has been obliterated by a housing estate that was built across the lower part of the hill. Beyond the houses the relatively recent A607 by-pass road cuts across halfway up the hill, and an extensive diversion is required to reach what had been the beginning of the Pingle. That is now marked by a cul-de-sac called Beverley Close (SP 6124.0920). Only someone who was familiar with the area many years ago would know that an old churchway had ever existed there.

I was certainly familiar with the Pingle, as I used it to traipse to and from the village junior school. I was walking up it with a school friend on our way home for lunch one sunny day in the early 1950s when I suddenly became aware of an airship hovering low over the top of Church Hill – it was as long as several of the houses crowning the hill. It had some kind of fin arrangement at the back and there was a gondola slung beneath it. It was huge, black and silent. Awe-struck, I turned to my school friend who was staring at it open-mouthed. I looked back, and it had vanished. We kicked up dust running up the Pingle to the top of the hill from where a wide vista could be obtained. There was no sign of the airship anywhere. I told my family about the exciting sighting but they informed me, correctly as I much later confirmed, that no such craft were flying in Britain at that time. Many years afterward, when researching the county for an article on unusual phenomena such as UFOs, I found that over a twenty-year period a few reported sightings had been made of "cigar-shaped" craft hovering over the immediate district around Church Hill. I did not consider the airship I had seen to have been an alien, extraterrestrial craft (I reckoned it would have had a hard job crossing the vacuum of outer space!) but it was clearly a mysterious phenomenon of some kind. I might not have seen a phantom funeral on my churchway, but I had seen a ghost of sorts.

OXFORDSHIRE
● 15. NOKE to ISLIP

Landranger 1:50,000 O.S. map, no.164 ("Oxford & Surrounding Area"). The village of Islip is situated 5 miles (8 km) north of Oxford and 2 miles (3 km) east of Kidlington. It is on the B4027, 1 mile (1.5 km) to the south of where that road crosses the A34.

The modern leisure route known as the Oxfordshire Way co-opts this mile-

Plate 35. A stile on the Noke-to-Islip churchway, with the path stretching beyond toward Islip.

and-a-half (2.4 km) corpse road, which makes for a pleasant walk across part of Otmoor, an area of Oxfordshire that has been described by various writers as a "curious area of almost wild fenlike desolation" and the "forgotten land" that is "cast under a spell of ancient magic". This despite being so close to the city of Oxford and its dreaming spires.

The pretty little village of Noke, one of the remotest on Otmoor, is at the end of a metalled lane that leads off the B4027 road. Part of the parish of Noke was granted to Islip by King Edward the Confessor, so the people of Noke paid their tithes there and were buried there. The route of the corpse road starts at a signposted stile (SP 5408.1305) off Noke's access lane at the extreme western edge of the village. It proceeds in a straight line to the north-west, passing through a tunnel of trees to a stile, beyond which the corpse road can be seen crossing broad open land with the tower of Islip church visible in the distance (Plate 35). The track eventually joins the B4027 just before it crosses the River Ray and enters Islip.

Islip is a large village that has lost some of its ancient charm, but it has a proud history, having hosted the palace of important Anglo-Saxon kings as well as being where King Edward the Confessor was born in 1004. Its present church, dedicated to St Nicholas, dates from the late twelfth century but it is thought that a Saxon church stood on the site previously. The church was largely rebuilt in the fourteenth century, the tower added a century later, and the whole fabric restored in Victorian times. Jonathan Swift tried but failed to become vicar of this church, which has much of interest in it. William Buckland, clergyman and the first professor of geology at Oxford, the man who first recognized the existence of what we now call dinosaurs, is buried in the churchyard. (This route was first brought to my attention by Lawrence Main.[26])

SOMERSET
● 16. HENTON to WOOKEY

Explorer 1:25,000 O.S. map, no.141 ("Cheddar Gorge & Mendip Hills West"). Wookey village is 2 miles (3 km) west of Wells on the B3139. Henton village is a little under 2 miles (3 km) further west along the same road.

This corpse way came to general attention in 1971 when the author Tony Roberts wrote an article about it after he had been informed of its existence by local people.[27] He saw it in the context of it being part of a "ley" (or "leyline" as the term now is), which he felt he could trace for 26 miles (42 km) across country. In fact, the route is locally reputed to have been a monks' path, possibly used by the brothers of Glastonbury or Wells, and it was certainly used as a corpse road (as Roberts acknowledged) by which the inhabitants of Henton and other settlements around it could take their dead to burial at the church in Wookey 2 miles (3 km) to the east (at ST 519.458).

The course of the corpse road passes through Yarley crossroads on the B3139 motor road (at ST 502.454). The old cross has now gone, but remembrance of it is kept in the name of Cross Farm, which abuts the intersection. The corpse road crosses a small bridge over a watercourse here, and goes along a narrow lane that gradually veers away to the north from the motor road. In less than half a mile (0.8 km) Monk's Ford on the River Axe is encountered (Plate 36). When Roberts visited this in 1971 he traced "some of

Plate 36. Monks' Ford, on the Henton-to-Wookey corpse road, Somerset.

Plate 37. The replica "Diamond Stone" near Monks Ford.

the old cobbled stones that once marked this ancient track . . . [which] run up out of the water to continue in a straight line along a raised, paved embankment which is now overgrown with grass and weeds . . . I could clearly see the remains of its broken flagstones showing here and there through the thin topsoil and grass".[28] This raised verge, marking the course of the original track, is on the right of the more recent lane as one approaches the ford from Yarley crossroads, and the exposed segment was about 600 ft (180 m) from the ford. I visited the place shortly after Roberts' article appeared and also saw the remnants of the old paving. These have now disappeared, for it seems the flagstones were used as packing around a nearby drainage ditch that was laid some time after Roberts' discovery.

Local folk had told Roberts about a "Diamond Stone" on which coffins were rested, and using a trowel he uncovered it. "The old 'Diamond Stone' was indeed situated in the centre of the track . . . and when we had uncovered it we found it was a small lozenge-shaped stone now covered with lichens and moss, " he reported. "There was no trace of a base or plinth anywhere around it; it was embedded firmly in the earth." This original feature also later disappeared, but in 1991 Wookey Parish Council placed a replica in the appropriate spot (Plate 37). A bronze plaque fixed to it gives the simple legend: "This stone replaces a coffin resting stone on the way to Wookey Church". The words are already faint and hard to read, and the replica Diamond Stone (ST 5060.4552) has itself almost disappeared among the weeds and grass.

A footbridge now crosses the river alongside Monk's Ford, and the course of the old corpse way continues through a field gate immediately facing the

Plate 38. A reconstructed segment of the Sweet Track at the Peat Moors Centre.

other side of the ford and diagonally across fields beyond, eventually connecting with Monksford Lane, which leads into Wookey. The church there is dedicated to St Matthew, and the present fabric dates from the thirteenth century, though it was heavily restored in the nineteenth century. It is thought likely that there was an earlier church on the site, as the original churchyard was circular in shape – as the church notes correctly state, circular churchyards are "often indicative of an early site". (This route was first brought to my attention by the work of the late Tony Roberts.)

● 17. SWEET TRACK

Explorer 1:25,000 O.S. map, no. 141 ("Cheddar Gorge & Mendip Hills West"). The course of the Sweet Track (shown as a fine dotted line on the 1:25,000-scale map) runs east of and roughly parallel to a minor motor road that links the villages of Westhay and Shapwick on the Somerset peat moors or "Levels" 5 miles (8 km) north-west of Glastonbury. The northern segment of the motor road (out of Westhay) is called Shapwick Road, the southern section is marked as Station Road. The Peat Moors Centre (open 2 April – 29 October) on Shapwick Road is situated next to the course of the Sweet Track.

It is only fitting that an entry in this sampler of Otherworldly routes should concern one of the oldest roads in the world. The Sweet Track (named after Ray Sweet, the man who discovered it) is a raised timber walkway dating to 3, 800 BC that has been marvellously preserved in the peat bogs. The actual walkway surface is made of oak planks laid end-to-end supported on a V-frame of crossed poles that in turn were driven into a pegged, pole structure on the unstable surface beneath. This plank walkway was designed to cross what was once a reed swamp to a ridge of high ground to the south. The Sweet Track was over a mile (1.5 km) in length and ran in "a remarkably straight line".[29] The feature has been the subject of a long archaeological study, and various finds have been made along its course, such as a ceremonial jadeite hand axe, but of special interest in the context of this book are some wooden pins. Made from yew, each of them had been shaped and polished to make them sharp. The only things archaeologists could compare them with were objects found at Neolithic burial sites that appear to have been fasteners for bags containing cremated remains. All traces of such bags and their contents belonging to the Sweet Track pins have dissolved in the peat bog over the millennia. Because of these finds, investigating archaeologists have suggested that the trackway may have been associated with funerary activities. If so, the Sweet Track would have been one of the first corpse roads in Britain.

Naturally, the Sweet Track cannot be walked today, but the Peat Moors Centre (at ST 426.414) has a reconstructed segment that can be examined (Plate 38).

SUSSEX (EAST)

● 18. RINGMER

Explorer 1:25,000 O.S. map, no.122 ("South Downs Way–Steyning to Newhaven"). The village of Ringmer is on the B2192 some 3 miles (5 km) north-east of Lewes.

Ringmer has had a long tradition as a place of burial – a Romano-British cemetery was found there, and evidence of Saxon burial has also been uncovered. Much later, in the fifteenth century, the church at Ringmer (TQ 446.125) was at the hub of churchways leading in from all directions. It is a good exercise to try to trace these on the map. One came in from eastern communities along Potato Lane, others from settlements to the south, as shown by extant footpaths that include a section of Roman road known as Week Lane, and another system of paths came down from the north, including a particularly direct footpath that can be seen on the map to come from Norlington Gate Farm (TQ 455.138). The only one checked in the field for this Sampler was a churchway path from the north-west that came via Ham Farm (TQ 439.122). The path is marked on the map as diagonally crossing a field to the south-east of the farmhouse. The old name for the field was "Footpath Field" but on the ground there is no longer any trace of this path – there is only a weathered wooden footpath sign hidden in a hedge where the corpse road would have met Ham Lane, a now surfaced motor road leading into Ringmer and directly to the church.

Ringmer has a few interesting claims to fame that should be mentioned in passing. The village sign depicts a tortoise: this is a reference to Timothy the tortoise, which lived in the village for half a century and was described by the famed eighteenth-century naturalist Gilbert White. The creature's shell is in the British Museum. There are a couple of interesting American connections too: the wife of John Harvard, founder of the famous university, was a Ringmer girl, as was the wife of William Penn, founder of Pennsylvania. (The fact that Ringmer church was a focus for churchways was first brought to my attention by Lewes archaeologist and historian, John Bleach.)

WARWICKSHIRE
●19. BRAILES

Landranger 1:50,000 O.S. map, no.151 ("Stratford-upon-Avon & surrounding area"). The village of Brailes (Upper and Lower) is on the B4035 between Banbury and Shipston-on-Stour, about 4 miles (6.5 km) east of Shipston, and 14 miles (22.5 km) south-east of Stratford-upon-Avon.

Visitors are often surprised by the large scale of the fourteenth-century church in Lower Brailes, but it was erected when the area had become prosperous owing to the wool industry. A rural backwater now, Brailes was once a place of significance. A stretch of medieval paving and (restored) steps nearby are known locally as the "Ninety-Nine Steps" (SP 314.396), though there is no signpost in the village indicating them and even some villagers have only a vague idea as to where they are (Plate 39).

The steps – and there are considerably less than 99 of them – are on a churchway that comes in toward the church (SP 315.393) from Upper Brailes directly to the west. Another branch joins it from the direction of the hamlet of Idlicote to the north-west, passing by the Norman motte and bailey known as Castle Hill (SP 308.401), around which Saxon finds have also been made. The route runs directly across fields (Plate 40) and through a few stiles before the Ninety-Nine Steps are reached and descended.

Plate 39. The so-called "Ninety-Nine Steps" at Lower Brailes, Warwickshire.

Plate 40. *Looking west on the Brailes churchway. Corpse roads were traditionally left as unploughed paths across fields, as is the case here.*

The old flagstone path at the base of the steps leads down to a footbridge across the narrow waters of the upper reaches of the River Stour. Brailes church comes into full visibility beyond the river as the route is followed across a field to another stile close to the church.

Brailes is on the lower slopes of Brailes Hill, a broad eminence visible from an astonishing distance to those who know to look for it: with a copse surmounting its brow, the hill is a true landmark. It is said that the ghost of a prehistoric man buried on the hill walks down Brailes high street at night. A Brailes tradition states that a right of way exists over Brailes Hill because the dead of the locality were taken to Bredon, a village situated 23 miles (37 km) due east at the foot of the thousand-foot-high Bredon Hill, another major landmark, which is crowned by the earthworks of an Iron Age fort. There is also a natural rock outcrop on Bredon Hill known as the Bambury Stones about which there is local lore, including witchcraft associations. This supposed corpse road was an oral tradition in Brailes until being written down and published in 1930.[30] It seems highly unlikely that there would be a corpse road of such length, but a Brailes elder, Alfred Woodward, claims that as a young man he traced the churchway westward through the Ninety-Nine Steps, past Castle Hill and all the way to Bredon.[31] Although no surviving footpaths and roads can nowadays be pieced together on the map to yield such a route, Woodward insists that in those places where there were no apparent paths to mark the route elderly people told him at that time (early in the twentieth century) that they could remember old tracks that had disappeared.[32]

In actuality, the churchway through the Ninety-Nine Steps seems simply to have served the communities in the countryside surrounding Brailes, but it is just possible that the piece of lore about the Bredon connection recalls some old, lost ceremonial way, or, perhaps more likely, prehistoric knowledge of an astronomical alignment between the two places. Researcher Brian Hoggard has pointed out that the equinoctial sun sets behind Bredon Hill when viewed from Castle Hill in Brailes, and this might have been viewed with significance in former times.[33] The Castle Hill motte and bailey is built on a natural hill, and so the viewing of the equinoctial alignment could have been noted long before Norman times. In addition, when a viewer sits at the Bambury Stones on Bredon Hill the equinoctial sun can be seen to set over another prehistoric earthwork on the Malvern Hills further to the west. So it is feasible that the Brailes tradition of a death road to Bredon is the relatively recent memory of the churchway mixed with the ages-old memory of a major equinoctial alignment through the whole region. It would doubtless have been ceremonially celebrated at places on its line such as Castle Hill or Brailes Hill, Bredon Hill, and the Malverns.

Such an idea is not preposterous, for Brailes Hill really does appear to have been on the cognitive map of prehistoric people in the region: the early Bronze Age stone circle called the King's Men at Rollright, 5 miles (8 km) away, was positioned so that the hill was due north, on a true meridian, from the site (Plate 41). This does not seem to have been some bizarre coincidence, because the stone circle was also placed precisely at the southernmost point from where Brailes Hill can be seen on the skyline.[34]

Before leaving this region, it is worth noting that the folklorist J Harvey Bloom wrote early in the twentieth century that "perfectly straight" corpse roads once existed at the villages of Fulready, Thornhill and Upper Ettington in the countryside around Stratford-upon-Avon, and that in Stratford itself

Plate 41. The Rollright stone circle.

such paths were "plentiful". One he cited was Shottery Road, which leads toward the riverside church in Stratford from the vicinity of Anne Hathaway's cottage. Stratford inhabitants who were elderly in Bloom's day knew the road as "Berrin Road" (that is, "Burying Road").[35]

WORCESTERSHIRE
●20. CRUISE HILL to FECKENHAM

Landranger 1:50,000 O.S. map. No. 150 ("Worcester & The Malverns"). The hamlet of Cruise Hill and the village of Feckenham are located 6 miles (10 km) east of the M5 and approximately 5 miles (8 km) south-west of Redditch, south of Birmingham.

The corpse road starts at a bend in a road (SP 008.638) in the hamlet of Cruise Hill, which is the close neighbour of another hamlet, Ham Green. It is easy to identify because a modern road sign marks it as "Burial Lane", reminding of its former use (Plate 42). A derelict chapel stands opposite the entrance to the road.

The course of the corpse road is preserved as a bridleway, and so is a clearly defined route. It initially has a tarmac surface where it passes a few buildings, but beyond a gate at the last of the houses it continues as a dirt track (waterproof boots are required in wet weather when it becomes an extremely muddy track). It leads to a ridge where footpaths connect at right-angles to the route, then descends as a tree-lined hollow way down a steep slope before reaching level ground (Plate 43). There are a few twists and turns, but overall the bridleway aligns fairly directly with Feckenham church, which lies almost due south. Further footpaths join here and there along the way – the whole district is crisscrossed with footpaths - but the broader bridleway itself should be followed. It curves round to the right (west), and gives a clear view of Feckenham church. A gate is reached alongside a four-way signpost, the left-hand arm of which indicates "The Green" and this direction is followed to reach Feckenham. The bridleway descends to a fording place in the river that intervenes before the village is reached. There is a footbridge here now and beyond this the route continues as a path alongside an old millhouse. This connects to a broad

Plate 42. The start of the corpse road from Cruise Hill to Feckenham cannot be missed with this clear road name sign.

earthen drive that becomes a metalled road coming in from the west to the village green. The whole route is about 2 miles (3 km) in length.

Access to the church (SP 009.616) is off the green. The church is dedicated to St John the Baptist and the present building contains masonry surviving from the thirteenth century, notably a set of remarkable pointed arches along one side of the nave. The present church tower dates from the fifteenth century, but this was preceded by one from the thirteenth century, so the church would have been clearly visible across the river and fields for over seven hundred years.

Although this corpse way presumably served both Cruise Hill and Ham Green, the map shows a footpath that may mark an additional route from the southern end of Ham Green: this goes past Dunstall Court and approaches the church from the north. Further research was not conducted on this route. (I first became aware of this corpse road through the work of Jo Sullivan.[36])

Plate 43. A hollow road section of the corpse road to Feckenham.

YORKSHIRE
● 21. GAYLE to HAWES

Explorer 1:25,000 O.S. map, no.OL30 ("Yorkshire Dales [Northern and Central Areas]").

Hawes is on the A684 between Junction 37 on the M6 in the west and Leyburn in the east.

Hawes is a tiny but lively market town in Upper Wensleydale, well appointed with shops, tea rooms, inns, and craft centres. Developed from a medieval settlement, it nestles amid high fells that provide an impressively scenic surrounding landscape. The clear waters of Gayle Beck tumble through it on their way down to join the River Ure, winding its way through the dale bottom below the town.

St Margaret's church in Hawes has a churchway leading to it from Gayle, half a mile (0.8 km) to the south. One interesting thing about this example is that it is paved with (modern) flagstones (Plate 44). It traverses an open area between Gayle and Hawes, and parallels the beck babbling busily along its rocky bed below. The path is known locally as Gayle Lane and forms a small segment of the modern long-distance leisure route known as the Pennine Way, which, like

Plate 44. *The paved churchway approaching St Margaret's church, Hawes.*

others of its ilk, tends to co-opt appropriate stretches of ancient pathways into its course.

This churchway offers a scenic and gentle stroll, and will probably be explored in reverse – that is, from Hawes toward Gayle – for those wishing to see only the feature itself. Others can include it in a day's walk along the Pennine Way. (This path was initially brought to my attention by Sibyl Webster, citing the work of Bob Swallow.[37])

●22. THE OLD HELL WAY: FRYUP to DANBY

Landranger 1:50,000 O.S. map, no.94 ("Whitby & Esk Dale, Robin Hood's Bay"). The small village of Danby is situated on the broad North York moors about 3 miles (5 km) south of the A171 between the towns of Guisborough and Whitby (on the east coast).

Danby and Fryup dales are parallel north-south valleys separated by a ridge called Danby Rigg. The southern ends of these valleys are closed. Fryup actually comprises two interconnected valleys, Little Fryup and Great Fryup (the furthest from Danby Dale): they are separated by a ridge that does not extend the full length of the dales, so allowing passage between them at the south. The southern termination of this incomplete dividing ridge bears the curious name of Fairy Cross Plain.

Danby's ancient church, dedicated to St Hilda, is situated in an isolated location within Danby Dale 2 miles (3 km) south of the modern village, which clusters around the rail track. The present church structure is the result of a number of restorations, not all of them sympathetic, but its fabric includes Norman and Saxon remains. The Anglo-Saxon settlement that surrounded the earliest church was not of any great size and the church seems rather to have been sited to form a central point for the broad moorland country all around. It was certainly the destination for a corpse road that was known locally as "The Old Hell Way".

Metalled roads now probably trace the original route taken by the corpse road from Great Fryup into Little Fryup, passing beneath Fairy Cross Plain, and leading to the start of the Old Hell Way itself, marked by a signpost at NZ 710.055 indicating "bridleway to Ainthorpe". The Old Hell Way does a zig and a zag on its way up

Plate 45. The deeply-worn Old Hell Way on Danby Rigg. None one of the stone marker posts to the right of the path in the distance.

the slopes of Danby Rigg, on the western side of Little Fryup Dale, its route being very deeply worn. It crests Danby Rigg and crosses over the flat summit of the ridge in a north-westerly direction; the track here is narrow and deeply engraved on the land (Plate 45). What look like "standing stones" are set at intervals along the right-hand side of the track: as the walker passes close to one of them, another appears over the skyline ahead. These stone posts or "stoops" were set up to mark the course of the Old Hell Way during wintertime, when snow settles on Danby Rigg. The posts had to be tall enough to project above even the deepest snowfall. From the last of the stone posts, before the Old Hell Way starts its descent into Danby Dale, St Hilda's church is for the first time distantly visible down below, set amid its dark ring of trees (Plate 46). The corpse road then becomes a steep trackway, in part crudely paved with rocks and in other parts a series of ruts, dropping down toward North End Farm (NZ 703.065). Beyond, a surfaced minor road continues the Old Hell Way's course to the church (NZ 696.063). It was over the Old Hell Way "that the inhabitants of the two Fryups carried their dead from the times of the early Danish settlers, and their bones now lie in what is spoken of as 'the old ground' in Danby churchyard, " wrote local man, Joseph Ford.[38]

John Christopher Atkinson was the vicar of St Hilda's from 1847 to 1900, and his grave is in the churchyard. In his book, *Forty Years in a Moorland Parish,* Atkinson tells of an old Fryup woman who had died "not so very long" before he took up his incumbency at Danby. The woman was known for keeping the "Mark's e'en watch", a reference to the "church porch watch" seership in which the forthcoming deaths in the parish were foreseen (see Chapter Two).

Atkinson recorded that when she was questioned after one of her vigils, the old woman announced her own death as among the "foredoomed ones". "And, " she added, "when I dee, for dee I s'all, mind ye carry me to my grave by t'church-road, and not all the way round by t'au'd Castle and Ainthrop. And mind ye, if ye de'ant, I'll come again."[39]

"Coming again" was the local term for haunting, and it was a deeply-held belief in the district that if a corpse was taken to St Hilda's by any route other than the Old Hell Way its ghost would come back to haunt the living. Atkinson stated that the corpse road "lay straight past her house", and this reinforces the connection between the British "church porch watch" seership and that of the death-road "precursors" of the Continent.

The old Fryup woman was possibly part of the tail-end of a tradition of witchcraft that had been deeply embedded in the region from the time of the first north European settlers. Relics of this tradition peculiar to the district are the carved "witch posts". These came about as result of what Joseph Ford referred to as a "mysterious ceremony" conducted by the Parish priest to nullify the believed evil influence of a local witch on a given dwelling, or even to perform "witch laying" if the spirit of a witch was thought able to penetrate the dwelling at night. After the ceremony, Ford reported:

... it was the custom of the Priest to cut the Roman figure X on the upright oak post which went up to the low ceiling. This was the main post of a partition which formed a short passage or corridor in the house that led from the outer door. This mark cut in the post by the Priest meant that the Witch's spell could not operate for evil any further into the dwelling or beyond this post.[40]

Plate 46. The final market stone on the Old Hell Way before it descends into Danby Dale. The church can be seen in the middle distance surrounded by a dark ring of trees.

Ford knew of many dwellings around Danby that still had these posts in his day, the first half of the twentieth century, and a few still do. An example can also be found in the Stang End Cruck House in the Rydale Folk Museum at Hutton-le-Hole, further south in the North York National Park.

Danby's Old Hell Way is a classic corpse road and is well worth visiting and walking, the more so because even local knowledge of it is seemingly beginning to fade – to judge by responses to queries made during fieldwork for this Sampler. It is also short: the length of the track from Little Fryup to Danby Church is just a mile (1.5 km) as the spirit flies, but it is naturally a little longer on foot because of its twists and turns on the slopes of the ridge. The Moors Centre in Danby is a good stopping point for maps, information and refreshment.

SCOTLAND

Corpse Roads

ARGYLL & BUTE

●23. *KILMORE

Landranger 1:50,000 O.S. map, no.49 ("Oban & East Mull"). Kilmore can be accessed from the A816 at Cleigh and Barran, approximately 4 miles (6.5 km) south of the coastal town of Oban, and is situated on a minor road close to the western end of Loch Nell. The church site is less than a mile (1.5 km) south of Barran at the entrance to Glen Feochan.

The church on the present site at Kilmore dates only from the nineteenth century, but the old church is situated to one side and behind the present building. This ruined structure dates from the seventeenth century, but is itself on the site of an earlier, thirteenth-century church. This is the earliest church building known of at the site, but the place itself is thought to have been a focus of Christian worship from the seventh century, when the region was evangelized by St Columba and his brethren from Ireland. Before even that, it is surmised that Kilmore was a pagan, Druidic sanctuary. Just behind the church there is a knoll whose Gaelic name means "Holy Hill"; according to legend, an angel appeared there and that was why the church was built. A holy well was discovered by the churchyard entrance; it is dedicated to the sixth-century St Beone. Altogether a most sacred spot.

Until recently, at least, there was knowledge of "the old ways" centring on the site of the ruined church (NM 886.250). In the early 1980s, researcher Michael Wysocki was told by an elderly local inhabitant that the church "lay at the centre of the ancient right-of-way tracks which crossed the mountains and came into the glens".[41] These old tracks converged on the church as if they were spokes attaching to the hub of a wheel. Wysocki was informed that "in the old days" far-flung communities conducted walking funerals along these roads to bring their dead to burial. Wysocki noted that one of the old tracks was still visible to the north, cutting through a ravine. Whether these old corpse roads belonged just to the seventeenth-century church, or went back to the thirteenth century was not ascertained. (I was first informed of this site by the work of Mick Wysocki, and it was field researched by him.)

WESTERN ISLES

●24. *ARDVEY to SEILEBOST, South Harris

Landranger 1:50,000 O.S. map, no.14 ("Tarbert & Loch Seaforth"). The Outer Hebridean island of Harris, off Scotland's north-west coast, is connected to the Isle of Lewis, its larger neighbour to the north, by a narrow isthmus at the community of Tarbert. As well as having an information office, shops and services, Tarbert has ferry connections with Uig (Isle of Skye). Harris and Lewis are directly connected by motor roads. The main town on Lewis is Stornoway on the north-east coast: this has ferry connections with Ullapool on the Scottish mainland, and it is served by flights from Glasgow, Edinburgh and Inverness – check with British Airways, Highland Airways, and British Midland Airways (bmi).

The original settlement on South Harris was on the fertile lands of the island's western side; the eastern side was settled only later, in the eighteenth century, when a chain of fishing stations was established. Early in the following century, landowners decided to raise sheep on the western side of the island and the people living there were cleared off the land. Most of the displaced inhabitants went to Canada. The rest went to the eastern side of Harris where they had to adapt to a different terrain and way of living. But they took their dead back to the western side for burial in the old graveyard at the community of Seilebost (NG 065.968). The funeral path traversed the island in a direct line for about 3 miles (5 km) from near Ardvey (Aird Mhighe) at the northern tip of the sea loch of Loch Stockinish, on the eastern coast, to what is now the motor road (A859) near Seilebost. Its course took it via the pass known in Gaelic as *Bealach creig an eoin*, "Pass of the Rock of the Bird". The course of the track is still marked on the Ordnance Survey map.

In 1995, artist Jill Smith reported on her experience of walking the route.[42] She set off from Bayhead, just to the north of Ardvey, and followed the track westward as best she could. Despite the impression given by the map, she found no continuous path on the ground and had to string together "bits of the path here . . . and there, following the pass and its streams". Along the first, eastern, part of the route Smith noted occasional flat rocks, which she understood to be coffin stones. This section of track is uphill toward the pass in the centre of the island, after which it gradually descends and is seemingly directed toward the mountains of Taransay, a small isle off the west coast of Harris. At points along this latter section there are well-constructed cairns (stone piles), which Smith learned had been used as sheltered stopping points by people going on ahead of the coffin so that they could have a bite to eat. She further observed:

The western part of the path is a definite raised track with water flowing on each side . . . It was only on the return journey that we became aware that the raised track was still there in a straight line most of the way across. Now no longer maintained, it has been cut across by water flows but is visible as straight rectangular lengths of clumpy heather about seven feet (2 m) wide. . .[43]

An aspect of the track that caught Jill Smith's artistic attention was the appearance of the hill called West Stocklett, which forms the northern side of the pass. Seen against the skyline it forms the "most incredible figure of a sleeping (or dead) Hag . . . hair streams back from her head which has a sharply delineated nose, sunken mouth and chin and a dark shadowy eye . . . In some lights she is hard and grey [as if] in rigor mortis; in others a dark black outline". The figure is acknowledged locally, though seen nowadays in the more general anthropomorphic guise of a "Sleeping Giant" rather than specifically as a hag. Nevertheless, other mountain ridges on Harris and Lewis are still referred to by *cailleach* ("hag" or "witch") names and it could well be that was the case with this ridge in more ancient times. (I first learned of this corpse road through the work of Jill Smith, and it was field researched by her.)

WALES

Churchways and Fairy Paths

BLAENAU GWENT
●25. *BLAINA
First Series 1:50,000 O.S. map, no.161 ("Abergavenny & The Black Mountains"). The village of Blaina is on the A467 about 3 miles (5 km) south of Brynmawr, which is in turn approximately 8 miles (12.8 km) west of Abergavenny.

A curious case of a claimed fairy funeral relating to the old church in Blaina (formerly known as Aberystruth) was recorded by Edmund Jones in the eighteenth century:

It was told to me that Mr Howel Prosser Curate of Aberystruth seeing a Funeral going down the Church lane, late in the evening, toward the Church, imagined it was the Body of a Man from the upper end of the Parish toward Brecon-shire, whom he heard before was sick; and thought was now dead; and going to be buried; put on his Band in order to perform the burial office; and hastened to go to meet the burial and when he came to it . . . putting his hand on the Bier to help carry the Corps, in a moment all vanished; and to his very great surprize and astonishment, there was nothing in his hand but the Skull of a dead Horse.[44]

The church site is in the centre of the village at SO 201.078; now occupied by the modern church of St Peter, replacing the "old church" of the same dedication. (I was first alerted to this fairy funeral case by the work of Frank Olding.[45])

●26. *HAFOD-y-DAFAL to LLANITHEL, Aberbeeg

Landranger 1:50,000 O.S. map, no.171 ("Cardiff & Newport/ Caerdydd a Chasnewydd"). The village of Aberbeeg is 5 miles (8 km) west of Pontypool and 1½ miles (2.5 km) southwest of Abertillery. It is situated on the A467 about 12 miles (19 km) north of junction 28 on the M4 and approximately 6 miles (10 km) south of Brynmawr.

Several instances of old Welsh lore bind fairy paths and churchways together, pointing up the spirit association with corpse roads discussed in Chapters Two and Three. It was said of Welsh fairies "very often they appeared in the form of a Funeral before the death of many persons, with a Bier, and a Black Cloth, in the midst of a Company about it, on every side, before and after it".[46] This was said to be quite a common sighting and was viewed as a death omen for it was "past all dispute that they [the fairies] infallibly foreknew the time of Men's death". It is possible that this was a vestigial memory of churchway seership. An instance of such a claimed sighting near Aberbeeg was recorded again by Edmund Jones:

> Isaac William Thomas . . . seeing, as it appeared to him, a Funeral coming down the Mountain; as it were to go toward Aberbeeg, or Llanithel Church. He stood in a Field by a wall which was between him and the high-way leading to Aberbeeg. When the Funeral, which came close to the side of the wall, was just over against him, he reached his hand and took off the black vail which was over the Bier, and carried it home with him. It was made of some exceeding fine Stuff, so that when folded it was a very little substance, and very light. He told this to several. I knew the Man myself, and in my youthful days conversed with him several times.[47]

There was some local wonderment that the said Isaac Thomas survived this encounter. Heritage Officer and County Archaeologist, Frank Olding, has determined the route implied in this account. The fairy funeral was seen at Hafod-y-Dafal (SO 2010.0364) on the top of the Cefn yr Arael mountain, which rises immediately to the north of Aberbeeg. "Its route to St Illtyd's [Llanithel] would have taken the funeral along the straight mountain path from Hafod-y-Dafal down into the valley at Aberbeeg itself and then up the 'Rhiw' (an old Welsh word for a road or track leading up a hill) at SO 2115.0149 and then up to St Illtyd's church."[48]

Although Llanithel Church (SO 218.020) is dedicated to St Illtyd, it was originally dedicated to St Heledd (or Hyledd), a seventh-century princess of Powys. The church's imposing mountaintop site stands above the village now known as Llanhilleth (a variant version of "Llanithel"), an anglicized form of Llanhyledd. Although much of the present building dates from around the thirteenth century, its origins are pre-Norman – there is a documentary reference to a church there as far back as the ninth or tenth centuries. Two very ancient trackways converged on the spot, and it is thought that at least one of these may go back to Roman times. St Illtyd's was also on a pilgrimage route from the Cistercian abbey at Llantarnam to the shrine of Our Lady at Penrhys in the Rhonnda Valley. There is a tumulus – an ancient earthen mound – close to the church that is thought to be a Norman motte, but was probably built over an earlier, prehistoric mound. St Illtyd's gradually fell out of touch with the communities developing down in the valley, which built new, local churches in the nineteenth century, and it became increasingly neglected, fell into serious disrepair and was ultimately declared redundant. More happily, the church has been restored in recent years and is now used as a venue for lectures, concerts and other events. The Friends of the church encourage people to visit it.

Llanithel appears to have been quite infamous for its active fairies. Jones records the case of Henry Edmund who though warned that the fairies there "sometimes took Men in the night and carried them insensibly into other places" decided to walk home at night. Sure enough, he "was taken up on the way, and carried so far as to the town of Llandovery" roughly 30 miles (48 km) away in a straight line over wild, mountainous country. The next morning, he was returned to Llanithel. This is remarkably reminiscent of today's so-called "alien abductions", and shows how deep the archetypal roots of such experiences can extend. (I was first alerted to this fairy funeral case by the work of Frank Olding.[49])

FLINTSHIRE
●27. HAWARDEN to GRESFORD

Explorer 1:25,000 O.S. map, no. 256 ("Wrexham/Wrecsam & Llangollen"). The specific section of this 7-mile (11-km) long churchway or monks' path that is dealt with below is situated in countryside between the A550 and A483 roads 5 miles (8 km) north of Wrexham and 2 miles (3 km) east-north-east of Caergwrle. Gresford is immediately to the north of Wrexham.

A corpse road used to come to the important church at Gresford (SJ 3465.5495) from Hawarden some 7 miles (12 km) to the north. The remaining fragments of this "monk's path" were traced through in 1989 and found to be "very straight".[50] What is probably the most accessible remnant of this route – a north-south stretch from SJ 329.587 to SJ 331.582 – can be reached from a stile on the south side of a minor road in front of Town Ditch Farm (SJ 329.589), a mile-and-a-half (2.5 km) east of Hope village.

To get onto the course of the corpse road the walker turns left immediately after climbing over the stile and follows the hedgerow to the corner of the field, then turns right to follow another hedgerow from there to a break where a plank bridge lies across a ditch. On crossing this, the walker turns left and walks for a few dozen paces up the edge of the field to reach a hedgerow – this marks the actual course of the old corpse road. Turning right (south) here, this hedge is followed to the end of the field where there is a steep dip down to a footbridge over a stream. Onward, keeping the hedge to the left and proceeding to the end of the next field another stream is crossed. There is a copse of trees at the crossing point, beyond which the hedgerow is now on the right of the path. It is important to bear in mind that it is the hedge line and not the path running alongside it that marks the exact course of the original corpse road (Plate 47).

The road had only been 3–4 ft (1–1.2 m) wide, and was made up of small stone cobbles placed tightly together and prevented from spreading by a retaining kerb. If this last stretch of hedgerow is examined closely, something of this structure can be detected beneath it. At the end of this section of hedgerow the present footpath, approximating the course of the corpse road, continues on across a large open field containing a small valley or gully, ultimately rising up to a stile on a country road, known as Cobblers Lane, on

Plate 47. A section of hedgerow actually growing along the course of the Hawarden-Gresford corpse road.

the far side. If this lane is walked a short distance to the left (east) a metal field gate is seen in the hedge on the right-hand side. A narrow gap next to this reveals a subtle depression that leads down into a valley. This is the continuing course of the corpse road, but is not now a public footpath (it was seen to be littered with rubbish during fieldwork for this Sampler).

All Saints' church in Gresford is set within a huge churchyard known as The Green. The church is an impressive building with much to see, including medieval stained glass. Its peal of bells is considered one of the wonders of Wales. (This corpse road was first brought to my attention by Laurence Main, [51] citing the work of R J A Dutton.[52])

GWYNEDD
●28. LLANYMAWDDWY

1:50,000 First Series O.S. map, no. 125, ("Bala and Lake Vyrnwy"). The route described here to Llanymawddwy church is a minor road that starts 1 mile (1.5 km) north-east of the village of Dinas Mawddwy, which is on the A470 1½ miles (2.5 km) north of Mallwyd, itself 11 miles (17.5 km) north-east of the town of Machynlleth.

One mile (1.5 km) along the road from Dinas Mawddwy to the small and remote community of Llanymawddwy there is a narrow turning on the right which leads steeply down to a bridge (SH 872.157) over the River Dovey (Afon Dyfi). Beyond the bridge this lane then bends left to follow the south-east side of the Dovey Valley, keeping the river on its left-hand side and paralleling the more direct road to Llanymawddwy, which continues on along the other side of the valley. The lane wends its way through beautiful mountainous landscape for about 3 miles (5 km) before re-joining the more direct road onward to Llanymawddwy. It was along this loop that people living in the scattered hill farms on the south-east side of the valley took their dead to burial at the church in Llanymawddwy.

Local man and country-walks author, Laurence Main, heard an oral account of two experiences along this lane that befell one Margaret Lewis (d. 1958). It was obtained from a member of her extended family. In the first incident, Margaret Lewis was walking home northward (in the direction of Llanymawddwy) along the lane one moonlit night after visiting a sick neighbour at the farmhouse of Troed-y-Rhiw, which abuts the lane (at SH 884.160). Passing the house named Esgairadda (SH 886.161)[53] she saw two robed clergymen leading a funeral procession ahead of her (Plate 48). It stayed in sight until it reached a now bridged ford across the stream of Nant Efall-fach (SH 891.166) where it vanished before her eyes. The next morning Margaret learned that the sick woman at Troed-y-Rhiw had died overnight.

Her funeral took place exactly as Margaret had foreseen it, including the fact that two vicars had led the procession – the vicar who served Llanymawddwy church happened to have another clergyman visiting him at the time who also took part in the funeral service.

On another occasion, Margaret Lewis saw a corpse candle *(canwyll corfe)*, a mysterious ball of light interpreted as a death omen, travelling between two houses, Ty-mawr and Ty'n-y-ceunant, further north along the lane and to its right-hand (easterly) side. It transpired that a few days later a woman died in childbirth at Ty-mawr and her corpse was rested in Ty'n-y-ceunant before being taken on to Llanymawddwy for burial. It would seem that Margaret Lewis had prophetic vision, what Scottish Highlanders call "second sight", and in an earlier time she would have been a seer of the corpse roads (see Chapter Two).

The church site at Llanymawddwy has ancient origins. The first documented mention of there being a church there appears in taxation records of 1254, but the sixth-century Breton anchorite, St Tydecho, is known to have had a cell and chapel there. Before even that early date, eighteenth-century accounts record that a now-lost pagan (Roman) memorial stone was discovered near the churchyard. Did corpse way seership in the area go back to such early times? (Information on the seership along this lane was first brought to my attention by Laurence Main.[54])

Plate 48. Part of the haunted section of the Llanymawddwy road where a prophetic vision of a phantom funeral was seen.

GERMANY

Corpse Roads, Churchways, and Spirit Routes

BADEN-WÜRTTEMBERG
● 29. *GOCHSHEIM and BAHNBRÜCKEN

These two tiny communities lie in countryside 30 miles (48 km) north-west of Stuttgart, and 20 miles (32 km) south of the picturesque city of Heidelberg. Gochsheim is on the L618 road 3 miles (5 km) west of Zaisenhausen, which is on highway 293 linking Karlsruhe and Heilbronn. Bahnbrücken is 2 miles (3 km) north-east of Gochsheim.

Studying a topographic map of the area, author and researcher Ulrich Magin noted a path marked Totenweg, "death road", between Gochsheim and Bahnbrücken. He visited the site and found the map-marked route to be a gently undulating field path that descended a mountain slope. At the bottom, it ends in a sharp angle.[1] Magin was unable to find any church, chapel or cemetery in its vicinity, but its name clearly indicates that it must be a fragment of a former corpse road.

As in Britain, such roads were given a variety of names, including Leichenweg (corpse road), Kirchweg (church road), and Hellweg (Hell or Hel road). This latter term is echoed in the former local name for the corpse road at Danby in Yorkshire (entry 22). (Field researched by Ulrich Magin.)

BAYERN
● 30. *ROTHENBURG o. d. TAUBER

Rothenburg ob der Tauber is situated just west of the A7 highway (also Euro-route E43) 60 miles (100 km) north-east of Stuttgart, 40 miles (64 km) west of Nurnberg, and 30 miles (48 km) south of Würzburg.

The north Bavarian town of Rothenburg o.d. T., overlooking the sinuous Tauber valley, is charming and remarkably well-preserved. With cobbled streets, ancient half-timbered buildings, and completely ringed by its walls, it was considered by nineteenth-century artists as the "epitome of Germanic medievalism". Naturally enough, artist and death-road expert, John Palmer, felt it was an ideal place to look for medieval death roads. The town's main church, the Gothic basilica of St Jacob, caught his eye. It dates from the fourteenth and fifteenth centuries (though it stands on the site of an earlier church dedicated to St Kilian), and contains a stone statue of the Virgin made in 1360 as well as stained glass from the same century. The church is also famed for its intricate altarpiece carved in 1505 by Tilman Riemenschneider. However, it was the long axis of the building that was of particular interest to

Palmer. He noticed that if it was extended eastward to the medieval town wall it intersects a gate by the White Tower (Weisser Turm). Extended in the other, westward, direction, it bisects a tower in the medieval walls where there is a death road, so indicated by its name, "Todtenwetn". This runs straight as far as the corner of the St Jacob's thoroughfare. Palmer observed that an unusual feature of the thoroughfare is that it passes underneath the choir of the basilica.[2] (Field researched by John Palmer.)

NIEDERSACHSEN
●31. WURMBERG, Hartz Mountains

The Harz are located approximately 50 miles (80 km) south-east of Hannover and 130 miles (220 km) south-west of Berlin. The Wurmberg peak is north-east of the town of Braunlage, from where the Wurmberg cable car or seilbahn can be boarded. Braunlage is on the B4 road about 12 miles (19 km) south of Bad Harzburg, and also on the B27 36 miles (58 km) north-east of Gottingen.

The Harz are associated in folklore with witchcraft, and witches were said to hold a major gathering on the Brocken, the tallest peak of the range, on Walpurgis Night (May Eve). The region generally held on to pagan beliefs tenaciously, and it was a hunting ground for the brothers Grimm when collecting their folktales. The Wurmberg ("Dragon Mountain") is the fourth highest Harz peak at over 3000 ft (914 m). The cable car is taken to the summit, and immediately to the north of the wheelhouse, a dead-straight, stone-paved pathway known as the Steinweg is encountered (Plate 49).

The Steinweg is aligned east-west. To the west it leads to a prehistoric stone ring (Ringwall). The exact date of this feature has not been established, but the best

Plate 49. A section of the mysterious Steinweg where it leads up to the summit plateau of the Wurmberg, Hartz, Germany.

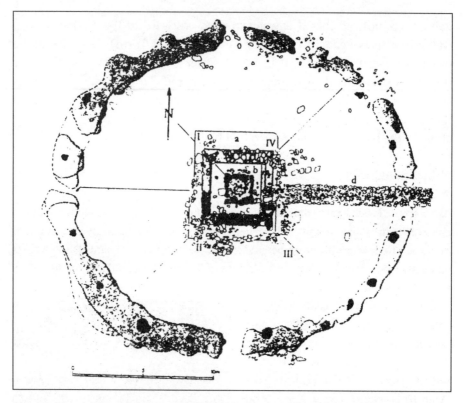

Fig. 13. Plan of the Ringwall on the summit of the Wurmberg, Hartz, Germany. The mysterious Steinweg is shown leading into the stone circle from the east (right).

interpretation is that it is an Iron Age feature on an earlier, possibly Neolithic, site. It consists of a central cist (a box-like stone grave) set in the ground surrounded by a circular area 80 ft (25 m) across defined by low stone walls in which there are four gaps or entrances at the cardinal points. The paved pathway enters through the eastern gap and goes through to the cist (Figure 13). Another Ringwall is situated six hundred paces away to the north-west, and the two sites are linked by another stretch of straight, paved pathway. This whole complex is on the summit of the mountain, which is thought to have been artificially flattened in prehistory.

To the east, the Steinweg leads from a series of broad but uneven stone steps known variously as the Pagan Stairs (Heidentreppe) or Witch Stairs (Hexentreppe) climbing up the edge of the summit plateau (Plate 50). Below them the stone path can be seen leading up amid the trees from far down the mountain's slopes.

The most remarkable factor about the stone pathway is that pollen

Plate 50. The Hexentreppe, Witch Stairs, on the Wurmberg.

analysis has shown it to date from between the eleventh and thirteenth centuries AD. In other words, it is a medieval route connecting to prehistoric places of the dead. The precise nature of that connection and how it came about is unknown, but it presumably indicates that the pagan, prehistoric associations with the stone rings were still alive in the medieval era. This must surely be what is reflected in the witchlore associated with the Harz in general, and the claimed longevity of paganism in the region.

The mystery stone path on Dragon Mountain is clearly a death road of some kind; a truly eerie Otherworld route. (This path was brought to my attention by the work of Ulrich Magin.[3])

NORDRHEIN-WESTFALEN
●32. *OBERKRÜTCHEN to ETSBERG (in Limburg, Netherlands)
The village of Oberkrütchen lies almost on the border with the Netherlands 22 miles (35 km) west of Monchengladbach, close to Düsseldorf. It is situated ½ mile (0.8 km) south of the A52.

A road leads south-west out of Oberkrütchen toward the border with the Netherlands and the Meinweg. This is an area of forest and heathland stretching across the German–Dutch border that was formerly strongly associated with witchcraft. It is now a recreational area, being granted national park status on the Dutch side. The road initially follows a slightly curved course but straightens within the Meinweg, where investigator John Palmer

143

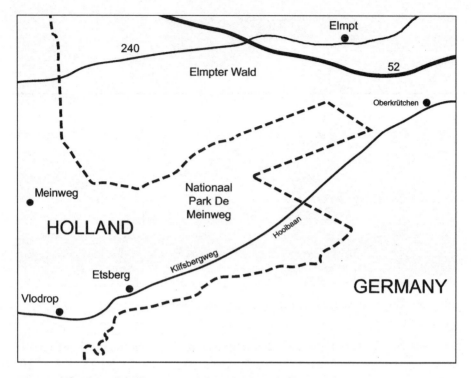

Fig. 14. The (simplified) course of the Oberkrütchen-to-Etsberg corpse road, which crosses the German-Dutch border.

found it was marked as a *Leichenweg*, "corpse road", on older maps.[4] The road passes on into the Netherlands, the border being marked simply by a red-and-white barrier pole (or was at the time of the field investigation in the 1990s). At this point the road now becomes known as the Hooibaan, derived from an old German term, *hew*, referring to tracts of land on the Meinweg where timber felling and sheep herding were not allowed. It continues in an almost straight line toward the Dutch village of Etsberg. Before reaching this place, though, the course of the Hooibaan meets a modern dual carriageway at a spot called De Kievit, formerly marked by a cross, beyond which it merges with a road called the Klifsbergweg, which leads into Etsberg. The entire length of the road is approximately 6 miles (10 km) (Figure 14).

Palmer's study of old maps and documents convinced him that the road passed on through Etsberg to the next village, Vlodrop, then a few hundred yards south to the hamlet of Kerkberg where Vlodrop's medieval church – and the mother church of the district – stood until the eighteenth century. (Field researched by John Palmer.)

IRELAND
Fairy Paths and Places

CAVAN
●33. MONEYGASHEL ROCK to GOWLAN CROSS

Discovery Series 1:50,000 O.S. map, no.26 ("Parts of Cavan, Fermanagh, Leitrim, Roscommon, Sligo"). This beautiful area is hard by the border with Northern Ireland and is very much off the beaten track. It is to the south of Lough Macnean Upper and the N16 highway. Access is via a country lane leading east off the R206 road, which itself runs south out of Blacklion. This village is on the Irish side of the border with Northern Ireland and its "twin" village immediately on the other side of the border, in Fermanagh, is Belcoo, situated on the A4 approximately 12 miles (19 km) south-west of Enniskillen. (Refreshment and lodging is available in Belcoo and Blacklion, and the museum of the Belcoo and District Historical Society in Railway Street, Belcoo, is recommended.) Gowlan Cross is just a few houses and a church clustered around a tiny crossroads 3 miles (5 km) south-south-west of Blacklion. It is on the modern long-distance leisure route known as the Cavan Way. Moneygashel is simply a hill and the general area around it (the "Rock" being a rocky tor on the hilltop).

An invisible fairy path supposedly ran from Moneygashel down to Gowlan Cross (H 066.335). The fairies came down to the crossroads in the form of

Plate 51. Looking inside the walls of Moneygashel's fairy-haunted Iron Age fort.

foxes, and once killed the chickens belonging to a man living at Gowlan. The man went up to Moneygashel, found their hole and smoked them out. The fairy foxes were never seen again, but they had their revenge because the man accidentally shot and wounded himself in the process of expelling them.

The whole area around Moneygashel was thought of as a powerful fairy locale – lights were seen on the rocky summit, and people kept their doors closed at night – but the key fairy point seems to have been the cashel (an Iron Age fort of the kind typically considered a fairy dwelling in former times) on the summit slopes. It is marked on maps as a small red ring at H 059.339. Though a ruin, its white, labyrinthine drystone walls still fully enclose its circular, grassy interior, and the entranceway is extant (Plate 51). The walls stand quite high in parts, and on one occasion a local man who was climbing on them was cast down "by fairies" and injured.[1]

The hill of Moneygashel was an important place for thousands of years, as is evidenced by a Neolithic tomb a short distance to the north of the cashel at H 0605.3415. Inside a low drystone wall abutting the monument stands an old, lone thorn tree, and it would almost certainly have been considered to be a fairy tree.

Such a prehistoric heritage at Moneygashel could be one reason why it was a noted fairy haunt, along with the fact that it overlooks the source district of the River Shannon. (This fairy haunt was brought to my attention by Dr Robert Curran,[2] who learned about it from local oral sources.)

CLARE
● 34. ATTYQUIN LOUGH, Banshee Path
Discovery Series 1:50,000 O.S. map, no.52 ("Parts of Clare, Galway"). The track leads off the left (west) side of the N18 highway opposite Attyquin Lough, 11 miles (17.5 km) north of Ennis town.

The term "banshee" is the anglicized version of the Gaelic *bean si* which literally means fairy woman, though some academics translate it more broadly as "Otherworld woman" and even as deriving from a folk version of the mythical Earth goddess or a nature spirit. Banshees are harbingers of death: fairy beings who for some unknown reason have ancestral connections to particular families.[3] When a person is dying it is said the ancestral banshee is heard by family members to wail somewhere in the vicinity of the house (though it is commonly held that the person who is dying does not hear it). She cries more often for male members of a family than its female members, and only at night or when daylight is fading. One description of a banshee cry by a claimed witness was that it was "the most awesome, unnatural sound".

Plate 52. The derelict house at the end of the Attyquin Lough "banshee path".

Generally, it is variously described as a drawn-out wailing, or roaring, or a lament or "keening". "In genuine folk tradition the wail of the banshee is imagined to consist of inarticulate sounds and isolated interjections only, unlike the lament performed by the human keening woman, which contained *ex tempore* verses in praise of the deceased to express the sorrow of the relatives and community at his demise" informs Irish folklorist, Patricia Lysaght.[4] The banshee is rarely seen, and so descriptions of her appearance are sparse and varied. She can be described as both young and old, though the image of a small, old woman predominates. There is general agreement that she has long hair – usually white or grey – which she combs when conducting her eerie calls. Her most commonly described apparel is a white and often hooded cloak. (Lysaght suggests that among other death associations, white relates to spirits or ghosts.)

The banshee path off the N18 road opposite Attyquin Lough north-east of Ennis is marked on the map at R 4185.9070, but its status as a right-of-way has not been confirmed. It is now largely re-worked as a farm track, and there are new metal farm gates at its entrance off the N18. It can be followed a short distance to and through a further gate, where the course of the track continues alongside the hedgerow before crossing a more open area. At the end of the track is a now derelict house amid trees (Plate 52). It possesses a distinctly sinister aura. The building is close to a small lake or pool (at R 417.910); this is marked and unnamed on the map but was once known as Katie McGuane's Lake. Although probably having once simply served the now-derelict house, the path can also be seen as connecting Attyquin Lough (known locally as Anna Griffey's Lake) and Katie McGuane's pool.

The association of this path with a banshee was recovered from old belief in the district by the County Clare-based folklorist and traditional storyteller, Eddie Lenihan. There is, or was, a banshee's rock in the vicinity of the path, though its precise position has not been identified at the date of this writing. Why banshee associations with this area should exist is not known; it could be because a banshee was heard when someone was dying in the now-derelict house, but the fact that the pathway passes a *cillin* could be another, or additional reason: a *cillin* (literally a "cell" or chapel) can be a burial place for unbaptized infants. Although one is marked on the map adjacent to the path (at R 4180.9075) there is nothing to see there now except an open area of undulating ground with some exposed rock surfaces. (This banshee path was identified for me by Eddie Lenihan.[5])

● 35. CAHERHURLY CROSSROAD

Discovery Series 1:50,000, O.S. map, no.58 ("Parts of Clare, Limerick, Tipperary"). The few, scattered buildings comprising Caherhurly are in a remote part of eastern Clare 28 miles (45 km) east of Ennis town and 4½ miles (7 km) south-south-west of Scarriff (at the western end of Lough Derg, itself a noted fairy area). Caherhurly is on the East Clare Way, a modern long-distance leisure route.

A house that was "in the way" of a fairy path at this location was recorded from oral sources by folklorist Meda Ryan.[6] Her elderly informant, Sonny Walsh, told her of the time Biddy Early, the famed Wise Woman of Clare, came to visit a sick person at Caherhurly. Biddy was travelling on a horse when she came to the crossroads at Caherhurly (R 619.797) and noticed a house in a field nearby. She commented that the house would not survive long, for it was "in a path". "But, " protested one of her companions, "that's a new house." "I don't care, " Biddy replied firmly, "that's in a path. That can't be there long." And after some years the house was indeed "knocked", an event witnessed by Walsh when he was a young lad. It was at this time he heard the Biddy Early story about the place. Sure enough, he and his friends were able to trace a row of whitethorns running south-east from the house: "The whitethorns were the mark of a fairy path".[7]

Difficulties were encountered in field-researching this Sampler entry. To begin with, Ryan mistakenly refers to the place-name as "Cahirburley". When this was sorted out and the location visited, no remains of a house could initially be found near the crossroads. Fortunately, it proved possible to meet Jimmy Walsh, son of Sonny Walsh, and he kindly explained the whereabouts of the site of the former house. It stands to the north-east of the crossroads, and is approached by a farm track at R 619.798 (not a right of way). All that remains of the house itself is a ruined stone wall forming one end of a much more recent cowshed. No sign of the row of whitethorns could be found, but it was noted that a line extended south-east from the house site could have led to a roadside fairy fort at R 628.795, a bare half-mile (0.8 km) distant (and marked as a red circle on the Ordnance Survey map).

The proximity of the house site to the isolated crossroads was also of interest because such places were notorious for being haunts of spirits, fairies, ghosts, witches, magicians, and even the devil throughout old Europe.[8] They were typically the burial places of outcasts such as executed criminals or suicides. During general enquiries made during fieldwork in the immediate district, a curious tale emerged by chance. We spoke to a woman who had lived in a house less than a mile (1.5 km) to the north of the crossroads. She had become ill and depressed while living there. She was restless one night and got up. In the living room at one end of the cottage she saw a line of small, shadowy figures materialize out of one wall and disappear through the opposite one. They seemed to be involved in a procession, and took no notice of her. She left the dwelling some time afterward. We visited the building, which was a small old cottage at one end (in which the apparition had occurred) with modern extensions. We spoke there to the woman's former partner, and he confirmed that she had told him of her experience, which he had thought might possibly have been some hallucination resulting from her ill-health. These individuals were not truly native to the district and were not to know that the old end of the building stood on a line that could be drawn from a nearby fairy fort to the crossroads. The course of a fairy path? In my enquiries into fairies and ghosts over the years I have on several occasions found what should be considered simply as old folklore manifesting in modern accounts of claimed actual experiences.

●36. DRUMLINE

Discovery Series 1:50,000, O.S. map, no.58 ("Parts of Clare, Limerick, Tipperary"). On private ground close to the hamlet of Drumline, which is east of the N18 highway and 3 miles (5 km) north-east of Shannon.

Drumline resident Mick O'Dwyer, one of Eddie Lenihan's local folklore sources (he insists that his claim of a chance contact with fairies when he was a young man is the memory of a real event and not a folktale), pointed out a physical path on his property that approximates the course of a fairy path connecting a local hill with a nearby fairy fort (Plate 53). There are prehistoric

Plate 53. Part of the path that is on the course of the fairy passage near Drumline, Clare.

standing stones on land flanking the path's course. "The only things that fly over this path nowadays are those, " O'Dwyer commented wryly during our fleldwork visit to him, pointing upward to an aircraft coming in to land at nearby Shannon airport.

The area around Shannon is rich in potential fairy forts, as the numbers of red rings marked on the Ordnance Survey map of the district testify. Lenihan showed me the sites of two such features set short distances back on either side of a road crossing the countryside between Drumline and Shannon. There is much mechanical earth-moving going on in this area, and one of the fairy forts was under threat of nearby workings while the other had been completely bulldozed away. One of the sites yielded another of those curious conflations of folklore and actual events: during the earth-moving operations there had been several accidents to workers on the site, including a fatal one, and an archaeologist involved died. Naturally, all this could be simple coincidence, but nevertheless it uncomfortably fulfils the deeply-held superstition that it was bad luck to interfere with or destroy fairy places. These two sites fall in line with the Drumline fairy fort half a mile away, but there is no known lore that connects them specifically. (The Drumline fairy path and fort sites were brought to my attention by Eddie Lenihan.)

●37. LATOON Fairy Tree

Discovery Series 1:50,000, O.S. map, no.58, ("Parts of Clare, Limerick, Tipperary"). The fairy tree stands 5 miles (8 km) south of the town of Ennis by the N18 highway, within the major roundabout and flyover complex at Latoon near the turning for the Clare Inn, between Newmarket-on-Fergus and Clarecastle.

This is a true story, a fairytale of a dark kind . . .

Once upon a time there was a solitary and venerable old whitethorn tree that stood prominently in the raised centre of a field, and though its branches slanted to the north-east in response to unnumbered years of exposure to the prevailing winds, it still managed to signal springtime with a crown of white blossom. Folklorist Eddie Lenihan knew it to be an important marker on a fairy path because the elder folk of the district, whose living oral folklore he often tape-recorded, had for many years told him so. It was where trooping fairies from Kerry were said to stop on their way to and from doing battle with the Connacht fairies to the north. Here, on their return, the fairies would rest, revel and rejoice if the battle went well, or mourn and lick their wounds if it had gone badly. Any human being approaching the tree at such times would risk being cast into an enchanted sleep, to awake only many years later.

The fairy tree *(sceach)* was a major co-ordinate in the psychogeography of the region, but the seasons rolled by, the generations passed, and mythic time almost imperceptibly faded into calendar time. In 1999, men came to build a major highway intersection all around the area where the little tree stood.

Plate 54. The Latoon fairy tree within its protective fence during the road construction.

Plate 55. The vandalised Latoon fairy tree.
(Eddie Lenihan)

Gigantic earth-moving equipment strode the earth, transforming the local lie of the land so that the old fairy tree no longer stood proudly up on high within a field but was left down in a machine-hollowed depression surrounded by the emerging structures of the intersection flyover. Worse was to come: the thorn tree was in the way of the planned route of the widened and re-organized highway. It would have to go. Alarmed, Lenihan lobbied public opinion locally, across Ireland, and further afield - even across the broad Atlantic. His efforts paid off, for though some laughed at him many more were concerned. The thoughtful Clare County Engineer made sure to work with his council and the road contractors to see that the tree was spared. So it was that by the end of 2001, though the old tree stood next to the refurbished highway and within the shadow of the flyover, it was surrounded by the protection of a stout wooden fence (Plate 54). The kind County Engineer had even arranged that an advisor be appointed to look after the tree's future welfare. At last, all seemed well. But dark forces were afoot . . .

In the night-time hours of an August weekend in 2002, [9] some sad person with chain-saw or slash-hook came and hacked off the fairy tree's blossom-bearing canopy and all its branches (Plate 55). Most people reacted with disbelief, horror, or anger when they heard of the deed. The kind County Engineer called it "wanton vandalism". Lenihan described the perpetrator in various stern ways, but he had presciently articulated the matter best in lines from a poem he had written many years earlier:

> Above the driving chain-saw's steely shriek
> Who can hear the whispering of a tree? [10]

Although severely damaged, it seems the fairy thorn might just possibly survive to blossom in some future year, and many hope that will be so. Whether or not one believes in the literal reality of the fairy lore associated with this hawthorn tree, these events provide a sobering metaphor for our times.

FERMANAGH (NORTHERN IRELAND)
●38. GORTAREE to LEGALOUGH (aka LEGOLIALOUGH)

Discovery Series 1:50,000 O.S. map, no.26 ("Parts of Cavan, Fermanagh, Leitrim, Roscommon, Sligo"). Accessed via a narrow lane (starting at H 101.368) signposted as a scenic route to the Marlbank Plateau off a country road running east from Blacklion (see Sampler entry 33) and to the immediate south of Lough Macnean Lower. After about 1 mile (1.6 km) up this – in parts – steep, narrow, winding lane, take a concrete-surfaced track off to the right (west) and follow toward Gortaree (ask at the occasional farmhouse if unsure of route). A bare ½-mile (0.8 km) before Gortaree, a dirt track at the gate goes left (south) off the concreted track. This track leads down to Legalough. Legalough and Gortaree are marked on the 1:50,000 map (without which these remote places are difficult to find). The lough is on private land and there is no automatic right of way; while it is probable that no one will mind occasional visitors, ideally permission should be sought locally. Ask at the Belcoo Heritage Centre for further information – see entry 33.

Plate 56. Looking down on the powerful fairy place of Legalough, on the border between Northern Ireland and the Republic.

Legalough is a small, circular body of water in a hollow on the Marlbank Plateau (Plate 56). The border between Northern Ireland and the Republic, between Fermanagh and Cavan, passes through the middle of it. The Marlbank Plateau is a secluded, remote area which is as close to fairyland as one can nowadays find, for there are many places associated with fairies dotted across and around it. The late George Sheridan, an educated man who was extremely knowledgeable about local lore, took the author and folklorist Bob Curran to visit the little lake there in 1995. He told Curran that the lough (at H 088.347) was always considered a particularly powerful fairy locale, and "until recently" traditional storytellers, the keepers of lore like himself, held gatherings there because they were always so inspired by the spirit of the place. Sheridan himself lived for part of his life at Gortaree above the lough (at H 088.352); this handful of buildings has now largely fallen into disrepair. As the two of them walked down to the little lake, Sheridan advised that they say "By your leave" as they proceeded.

Sheridan maintained that a fairy path led from the plateau, past Gortaree, and down to the lough. Only a few clues were given as to its exact course: it lay "in a fold of the land" and a part of its course approximated a segment of the border line. The only way this description can be accommodated is by assuming that at some point the fairy path must have run alongside the lower part of a stream that enters Legalough from the east. (Information on this site was imparted to me by Bob Curran, citing George Sheridan.)

● 39. HANGING ROCK, Blacklion
Discovery Series 1:50,000, O.S. map, no.26 ("Parts of Cavan, Fermanagh, Leitrim, Roscommon, Sligo"). This is a scheduled natural heritage site 2 miles (3 km) east of Blacklion, Cavan, on the country road running along the south side of Lough Macnean Lower, a short distance beyond the turning to the Marlbank Plateau described in the previous entry. There is a pull-in for a car and an information board (which gives natural history information, and some lore, but does not mention the fairy connection).

This site is a fairy glen if ever there was one, with its gurgling, tumbling stream amid the green gloom of the dense trees clustering at the foot of the dramatic cliff of Hanging Rock (H 110.365), which forms part of the northern edge of the Marlbank Plateau. It is a landmark when approached from either direction along the country road that passes beneath it.

The glen is known as the Claddagh Glen and the stream is the Claddagh River. The fairy path was said to run along one bank of the river (fairies could not cross running water) which emerges in an obscure fashion from rocks at the base of the Hanging Rock cliff-face. A pool has formed where the water

Plate 57. The haunted rock pool in Claddagh Glen, Fermanagh, Northern Ireland.

emerges, and this was considered a particularly haunted spot to be avoided at night (Plate 57). A few feet above the point where the little river emerges is a cave through which the fairies disappeared into and reappeared from the cliff face (Plate 58). The fairies came and went along their riverside path, and used it – among other practices – for fairy funerals, a spectral phenomenon that the area in general was noted for. Legend states that an ancient chieftain, Donn Bin

Plate 58. The fairy cave in Claddagh Glen, entrance to the Otherworld.

Maguire, rode his horse into the cave and was never seen again. Peering into the mouth of the cave the waters of the river can be seen stretching back into the interior darkness. This river is in fact the same one that flows through the spectacular Marble Arch Caves a few miles away and passes underground to this point of emergence. It is this subterranean characteristic that imbues the River Claddagh with its Otherworld associations.

The Ulster Way, a modern long-distance leisure route, uses the course of the country road that passes by the glen. Signposts indicate the way to the Marble Arch Caves, which can be visited between March and September. (The fairylore of Claddagh Glen was brought to my attention by Bob Curran.)

KERRY
●40. KNOCKEENCREEN, Brosna

Discovery Series 1:50,000, O.S. map, no.72 ("Parts of Kerry, Cork, Limerick"). Knockeencreen is an isolated former farmhouse (and now a cowshed) 6 miles (10 km) south of Abbeyfeale. The N21 highway runs 1½ miles to the west, and the village of Brosna lies 3 miles (5 km) to the east.

The old farmhouse of Knockeencreen (R 0834.1760) stands on a fairy path. The place can be glimpsed in passing through a farm gate on a sharp corner of a narrow dirt track. There is little to see, for the old building is now

Plate 59. The interior of the Knockeencreen building, showing light coming in through the front (north) door on the left, and the recess of the back door opposite it, on the right.

being used as a cattle shed and is in any case on private land and should not be visited or approached.

The last inhabitant of the place, when it was a dwelling, was Tadgh Horan, who died early in the 1980s. Fortunately, Eddie Lenihan managed to interview him and record on audiotape the story of the house before the old man's demise. The house had been built by Tadgh's grandfather after the Potato Famine (1846–50), and his father had been born there, as had Tadgh himself. When grandfather Horan lived there a curious and unfortunate phenomenon presented itself. About every three years he would be awoken in the night by a hissing sound rather like meat frying in a pan. Apart from locating the source of the sound as being near the ground in the general area of the back door, he could never find anything tangible. On the morning after each such occasion, Horan would discover that one of his cows was dead.

One day an old travelling man – a tinker or gypsy – stopped by and fell into conversation with Horan, who mentioned his recurring, costly problem. The old tinker looked around and informed Horan that his house was situated "in a fairy path". Knockeencreen was "in the way", "in a contrary place" or whatever other term one wanted to use. The house is oriented to the compass points, and the front faces north. The front door is exactly opposite the back door (Plate 59). It transpired that the building stands on a north-south line between two hills, a line that forms the course of a fairy path. The old travelling man advised Horan to keep the doors slightly ajar at night. This he did, and the trouble ceased.

Tadgh Horan was at pains to emphasize to Lenihan that the house truly was situated between two fairy hills and so on the direct course of the fairy path that connected them. At the time of his

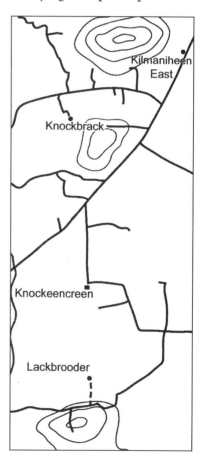

Fig. 15. The relationship of what was formerly the house at Knockeencreen with the road and the hilltops to north and south.

interview with the old man Lenihan did not get round to checking whether this was simply a general notion or a geographical fact, but during field and map research for this Sampler entry we were able to confirm that the building does indeed sit precisely on a line drawn between hilltops to its north and south. The spot height of the nearly 700 ft (215 metre) summit of the northern hill is at R 0840.1940 near Knockbrack, and that of the 800-ft (250 m) high hilltop to the south is at R 0830.1580 near Lackbrooder. Furthermore, a part of the northern segment of the fairy path's course falls along a length of dead straight track that leads up to the farm gate, which the north front of Knockeencreen faces (Figure 15). If this was in old China it would be said that the building's *feng shui* was bad, and would bring nothing but misfortune for anyone living in it. As observed in Chapter Three, there are curious similarities in spirit lore from one end of the landmass that is Europe and Asia to the other.

●41. *KNOCKNAGASHEL

Discovery Series 1:50,000, O.S. map, no.72 ("Parts of Kerry, Cork, Limerick"). The village of Knocknagashel (sometimes spelled as "Knocknagoshel" and both anglicized versions of Cnoc nag Caiseal) is located 1 mile (1.5 km) to the west of the N21 highway, 5½ miles (9 km) south-west of Abbeyfeale.

A local informant told Eddie Lenihan about the building of a particular public house just under 3 miles (5 km) north-east of Knocknagashel. When work was under way on it, the builder was warned by a passing stranger, "You're building the house on a path. Don't build it there . . ." The builder took little notice and the work continued. When it was finished, the man and his family moved in, but strange things began to occur: blankets would be pulled off beds by unseen hands, and strange, shadowy figures were seen around the house at night. "The fairies were all the time at the same house, " Lenihan's source told him. In the end, the house owner called in a priest to bless the place. As the priest went round the house "a bit of a closet" was found in a wall, and the priest stated that was where the disruptive entities lodged themselves.

The building was actually on the line of a "Mass path". These are, essentially, the Irish version of churchways. They are popularly associated with "Mass rocks", which were natural rocks in isolated locations used as altars for secret Catholic worship during the seventeenth and eighteenth centuries when attempts to suppress the religion were made by English Protestantism. After the worst of the suppression, Mass paths led to Catholic chapels or "Mass houses". In the nineteenth and early twentieth centuries Mass paths were used by people effectively as thoroughfares not only to get to church but also to access school and shops, and to visit friends. The walk to and from Mass was typically a social event as friends and neighbours met and talked en route. The linkage in this case of a fairy and a Mass path highlights the recurring and deep-rooted confusion in folklore between fairies and the dead, similarly exemplified in some of the Welsh entries described earlier.

The locations of both Mass rocks and Mass paths are rapidly being forgotten and lost, but some local history groups are attempting to catalogue them where possible.[11] (The pub location was researched by Eddie Lenihan.)

MAYO

●42. CLOONAGH

Discovery Series 1:50,000 O.S. map, no.32 ("Parts of Mayo, Roscommon, Sligo"). Cloonagh is a scattered hamlet 3 miles (5 km) north-west of Charlestown, which is on the N5 highway between Swinford and Ballaghadereen. Access to the hamlet is via country roads out of Charlestown, passing through Cully Cross Roads (G 453. 055).

The starting point for this entry was a reference in the Folklore Commission Archives at University College, Dublin, to "an ould fairy passage" that affected "Billy Brennan's house" at Cloonagh. Brennan found that his cattle were getting sick and dying. The matter grew worse until a disembodied voice told him to stop throwing out dry ashes and to shift the position of his gable (roof end). This account had been written down in the

Plate 60. The former "Billy Brennan's" house at Cloonagh, County Mayo. It had to have its gable end modified to stop it protruding onto a fairy path.

1930s, and referred to a claimed incident of unknown earlier date. It was not a lot to go on, especially as Cloonagh is well spread out with no clear centre. Fortunately, field enquiries led to Sean Haran, a born-and-bred local man who knew the tradition of the fairy path. It seems that it was understood to run in a roughly east-west direction through the area and was associated with a local fairy fort (marked on the map as a red circle at G 4465.0530). Mr Haran stated that the path ran from this fort to another one that is considerably smaller and is unmarked on the map. Subsequent fieldwork failed to identify this second feature. Part of the course of the otherwise invisible fairy path was supposedly once marked on the ground by a physical pathway running east from the main fairy fort. As far as the informant knew, this track had now disappeared.

"Billy Brennan's house" was securely identified (Plate 60) and, unlike other buildings said to stand on fairy paths studied for this Sampler, it is in good order, having been well refurbished. It is a family's private dwelling and so is not to be visited or approached by enquirers. For that reason no specific information on its location is given here.

WEXFORD
●43. KILCOWAN Fairy Path
Discovery Series 1:50,000 O.S. map, no.77 ("Part of Wexford"). The course of the fairy path approximates that of a track off the south side of the R736 road between Bridgetown and Duncormick at grid reference S 962.101. The locale is just a few miles from the south coast, and about 9 miles (14.5 km) south-west of Wexford town.

A 1935 account in the Folklore Commission Archives at University College, Dublin, tells of a fairy path that supposedly ran alongside "the old mill race" in an area of southern Wexford known as the Barony of Bargy. No further geographical information was given in the report, so there was even less to go on as a basis for fieldwork than was the case for the previous entry. Fortunately, a few hours' work at the public library in Wexford identified the location as Kilcowan.

Kilcowan is little more today than an old mill and a farm. The mill (S 961.099) is no longer used, but in its day it was the only one around that could grind maize. It is on a track that has obviously been widened and improved in recent times (Plate 61). During fieldwork, Mr John Codd of Kilcowan was able to show us the mill race, now but a trickle running along a ditch by the side of the road. If the line of the mill race (and thus the fairy path) is extended through the mill it passes onward through a mound (marked as "Motte") behind an ancient ruined church less than half a mile

Plate 61. The old mill race is now the ditch on the left-hand side of this lane, which marks the course of a fairy path. The view is from the direction of the former mill at Kilcowan, Wexford.

(0.8 km) distant. Mr Codd confirmed that during his long life the mound was always considered to be a rath, or fairy fort.[12] More or less on this line, between the rath and the mill, lies another ancient, moated earthwork that Mr Codd said also had always been known as a rath. The track leading to the mill continues onward to pass all these sites.

Mr Codd had not heard of a fairylore association with the mill race but mentioned that there was a bridge over the adjacent river that was said to be the haunt of a banshee. The 1935 report also referred to ghostly figures seen down by the nearby river.

NETHERLANDS

Death Roads and Spirit Routes

FRIESLAND

● 44. *RIJS-WYLDEMERK to HARICH

This area is in the remote south-western corner of this northerly Dutch province, near
the shores of the Ijsselmeer, the shallow lake north of Amsterdam formed from the old
Zuider Zee. It lies about 23 miles (37 km) south of Sneek, which is on the A7/E22
highway that goes north out of Amsterdam and crosses the Ijsselmeer. Leave this road
at junction 17 and follow the N359 south to Rijs.

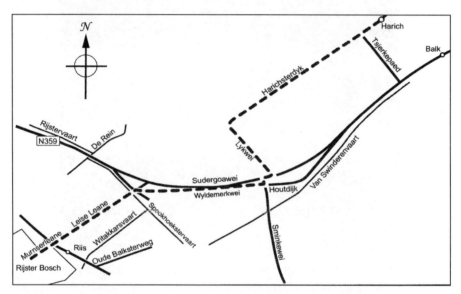

*Fig. 16. The (simplified) course of the Rijs-Wyldemerck-to-Harich map corpse road
or Lykwei.*

Taking as his starting point the woodland of Rijster Bosch, next to the
village of Rijs, researcher John Palmer discovered two examples of routes
with Otherworld associations (Figure 16).[1] A straight road to the north-east,
Leise Leane, is followed for almost a mile (1.5 km) from the wood, passing
Rijs and a few side roads, to a slightly staggered crossroads known as Wite
Brege ("White Bridge"). Immediately before this crossroads a canal is
crossed known as Spookhoekstervaart ("Ghost corner"). Stormleane runs
north-west (left) at the crossroads and Leise Leane runs south-east (right),
parallel to the dyke. These are presumably the remnants of what had been a

Dutch spook road *(Spokenweg)*. As discussed in Chapter Two, this was a name given to Dutch corpse roads that were deemed to be haunted and so unsafe to travel on at night.

A short distance straight on beyond the crossroads, at the next turning on the right, a road called Wyldemerkwei is arrived at. This runs east closely parallel to the N359 highway to its left (north), passing Wyldemerk. This area of lakelets and countryside was in olden times a *weerstal,* a sacred site and gathering place. After a little over a mile (1.8 km) the Wyldemerkwei comes to a crossroads with Sminkewei. Turning left (north) here and crossing an intersection with the N359 leads to the beginning of the medieval *Lykwei* (so named on large-scale maps). After an S-bend, this proceeds north-westerly in a straight line for just over half a mile (0.8 km) before turning right (northeast) onto Harichsterdyk. Before reaching this point, the *Lykwei* passes a farm called Spitâel. This name preserves the memory of a wooden chapel belonging to the Order of St John that was burnt down in 1487, during a period of local strife, with some loss of life. Later, mysterious lights were seen to rise from the chapel ruins that people interpreted as being a spiritual sign. A new chapel was built and holy relics placed within it, and a series of miraculous cures were said to have taken place there. The original chapel had stood on the site of a (probably Cistercian) wayside shrine. In the sixteenth century, however, Catholicism was outlawed in Friesland.

Harichsterdyk is aligned on the church tower in Harich, one-and-a-quarter mile (2 km) away. Shortly before Harich is reached, a road called Tsjerkepaed, a version of *Kerkpaden* ("church path"), joins on the right. The name "Harich" means hallowed place, and the church stands on raised ground surrounded by the churchyard.

"*Lykwei*" is the current Friesan spelling of *Lyckwei* – corpse road. Names with similar meaning that occur for features in various other parts of the Netherlands include Dooienstraatje ("death road"), in Oosterhout, North Brabant; De Dodedijk ("the death dyke") in Zuidwolde, Gronigen; De Dodesteeg ("death alley") in Wijk bij Heusden, North Brabant, and DeLijkenweg ("the corpse road") in Fredericksoord, Drenthe.[2]

NOORD-HOLLAND
●45. WESTERHEIDE, HILVERSUM
Westerheide is situated between Hilversum and the little town of Laren 3½ miles (5.5 km) to the north-east. It is open heathland on the northerly side of the N525 road. Opposite, on the other side of the highway, is St Janskerkhof (St John's cemetery). The whole district is a recreational area, and it is easy to pull off the main highway.

This is probably the easiest and best place to go to view Dutch *Doodwegen*, death roads. The heath is dotted with prehistoric burial mounds, and cutting for a few miles across it are three startlingly straight, well-kept pathways (Plate 62). These are the Doodwegen, a few miles in length, now maintained as leisure paths for walking and cycling. They converge toward a chapel at St Janskerkhof, which is located on raised ground. The cemetery is still in use, and the existing chapel is not particularly old, but may have replaced an earlier one. Two of the death roads are medieval, and the other dates from 1643. When they were being used for transporting the dead to St Janskerkhof they variously served the communities of Bussum, Ankeveen, and 's-Graveland. The paths have white, well-packed surfaces as they approach St Janskerkhof, but they become simple dirt tracks disappearing among trees the further they are followed in the other, westerly, direction. (I was first alerted to the existence of these death roads by the work of John Palmer.[3])

Plate 62. One of the Dutch Doodwegen or death roads on Westerheide, near Hilversum. The view is toward St Janskerkhof cemetery.

NEW WORLD

AUSTRALIA

Dreaming Tracks ("Songlines")

NORTHERN TERRITORY

●46. *WINBARAKU to DADA-KULANJU

"Winbaraku" is the Aboriginal name for Blanche Tower, a hill in the western MacDonnell ranges, very approximately 200 miles (320 km) west-north-west of Alice Springs in the very heart – the "Red Centre" – of the Australian Continent. The route proceeds northward from Winbaraku for about 200 direct miles (320 km), though on the ground the full route is closer to 300 miles (480 km) in length according to its eminent field researcher, the late Charles Mountford. The region that is traversed by the dreaming track is located about 200 miles (320 km) to the west of the Stuart Highway (which cuts through the middle of Australia from the north to south coasts). For non-Aborigines, it is about as remote a region as it is possible to imagine, and then some.

From a non-Aboriginal perspective this is possibly *the* classic "songline" or dreaming track. For it was following his 1960 journey along this route that anthropologist Charles Mountford was able to alert non-Aborigines to the existence of such features – or "totemic geography", to use his phrase. Reading his account allows non-Aborigines to get a more detailed idea of what a "songline" is actually like, a really up-close view of one, and that is why this entry reviews Mountford's journey.[1]

Mountford's guides were members of the Ngalia and Walbiri (Walpiri) peoples of central Australia. He lauded their considerate treatment of him and acknowledged that it was almost entirely due to them that he was able to make "such a difficult journey over that trackless and uninhabited country".[2] The Aboriginal elders felt that the course of the dreaming track and the dreamtime knowledge it contained would be best preserved with the anthropologist as the normal transmission of secret tribal knowledge to the young men of the tribe was being disrupted by the influence of non-Aboriginal culture.

The dreaming track is that of Jarapiri, the Snake Man (a version of the Rainbow Serpent), and his companions. The birthplace, or emergence point, of Jarapiri was Winbaraku, a distinctive twin-peaked hill where other dreamtime beings also emerged. From there, the route passes through thirty-five sacred, totemic sites (Figure 17). Mountford was able to map its course

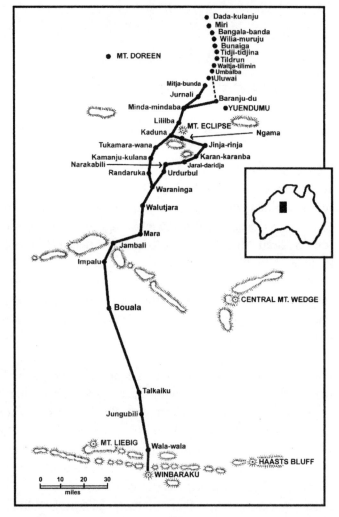

Fig. 17. A general plan of the course of the Jarapiri dreaming track. (After Charles Mountford)

and noted that in many places a precise route was followed, apparently known to the tribal peoples for unknown ages.

The first site out from Winbaraku is Wala-Wala, a gap in a ridge where the wood-gall people, the Wanbanbiris, conducted a short ceremony with flaming torches of eucalyptus leaves as the Jarapiri party started out on its dreamtime journey. The next site, Jungubili, about 18 miles (29 km) further on, is a totemic place near parallel lines of drifting sandhills that stretch across Australia for hundreds of miles. According to the Aboriginal song belonging to the site, "The meandering tracks of the snakes/become the drifting sandhills". The third site along the route from Winbaraku is Talkaiku, a bowl-shaped hollow in the sandhills where Jarapiri and his companions camped on their primordial journey. The totemic place after that is Bouala, 70 miles (112 km) out from Winbaraku. Here Jarapiri painted himself for a ceremony, and he shed his skin. That is now the claypan; some of the cracked and peeling mud on its surface were Jarapiri's scales. Dead trees on the claypan were snake-women of various kinds, and limestone deposits on its surface were the ashes shed by the burning torches of the Wanbanbiris. The following totemic places mark the dreaming track further north along its course to a point where the party broke into two groups:

> *Impalu.* Desert oaks here were the sons of Jarapiri. Mountford's guides showed him that the song for this place consisted of the words "Bai, bai, Kara, bai, Kara" chanted repeatedly.
> *Jambali.* This is a spring, and home of the young snake-woman, Jambali, and her child. On reaching this point, Jarapiri took her for his wife and briefly dragged her along the ground, forming what is now a short creek.
> *Mara.* Jarapiri saw the dog Malatji dig a hole beneath a eucalyptus bush and settle into it to sleep, causing him to sing a song that Aborigines following the route sing at the site. The bush is still there and the skeleton of a desert oak is Jarapiri.
> *Walutjara.* This place is a soakage or waterhole in a gap in a rocky ridge. A series of small rock outcrops or "reefs" going up a hillside are the tracks left by the Jarapiri party on its way to the soakage. There, the Wanbanbiri men performed a fire dance, and one of them danced with Jarapiri. The place has two songs belonging to it that relate to these dreamtime events.

At Walutjara, Mountford's Ngalia guides became uncertain as to the position of the next sacred site or of the songs that belonged to it. When Mountford asked the reason for this, he was told that their "line of songs" finished there and that those belonging to the remainder of the totemic route were the property of the Walbiri people to the north. This evidence suggested to Mountford that the finishing place of the "line of songs" belonging to a mythical route taken by dreamtime beings can act as a tribal boundary. Thus the notion of "songlines" was formed. Mountford had to make a round-trip detour of a 100 miles (160 km) to Yuendumu (an Aboriginal community that still continues the tradition of Aboriginal painting) to seek suitable Walbiri guides. He continued on his journey with them to the next totemic place on the route. This was Waraninga, where the snake-women danced and Jarapiri sang – both forms of expression repeated by those subsequently following the dreamtime track.

After the ceremony at Waraninga, the Jarapiri party split into two groups. One, consisting of snake-women, death-adder and another snake, Kamanaba, headed off northward while the rest set out in a north-easterly direction. The first group created the following totemic sites as it proceeded alone:

Randaruka. This is a low outcrop of rocks containing a deep spring. Two male snakes who lived in the spring were captured by the party and forced to carry Kamanaba. The one song associated with this site tells of this event.

Kamanju-kulana. Here a solitary desert oak marks where Kamanaba, carried ahead of the others by his press-ganged reptilian porters, stood on his tail to look back for the rest of the party. When everyone finally arrived, the snake-women sang a song that now belongs to the place.

Tukamara-wana. This is another waterhole amid a rocky outcrop. Here the members of the party painted white lines on their body for a ceremony. They left residues of the body-paint material behind, and this became a deposit of white ochre that was still being used as a source for ceremonial body decoration by Aborigines in Mountford's day. A single totemic song attaches to this site.

The other group, which included Jarapiri and his snake sons, the dog Malatji, and the Wanbanbiri people among others, created six totemic places as they went on their way to the north-east.

Urdurbul. This is a spring in the middle of a level plain. Here, Jarapiri and the Wanbanbiri men performed a ceremony during which burning leaves fell on the old snake man. In a fit of pique he went on alone to the next site, Nerakabili, leaving the others to catch up with him while he nursed his burns. Two songs attach to Urdurbul, one of which consists solely of spitting sounds, mimicking the noises made by the hare-wallaby man, Jukalpi, when he became scared by Jarapiri's outburst of anger. Mountford found the body-decorations for the main ritualist to be both colourful and complex, so his guides explained the meanings of the various images to him. For instance, a major visual component consisted of a long meandering line of red, beginning on the left leg, extending up the left-hand side of the body, over the head-dress, down the right leg, finally twisting back to end at a disk in the centre of the abdomen. This, Mountford learned, represented Jarapiri, the disk being his head.

Narakabili. This is a low, rocky rise with fig trees growing on it. A rock outcrop here was once the body of the old snake-man, Jarapiri, and rounded boulders nearby had been his sons. Two songs attach to the site, and again Mountford noted that the body decorations created here were complex and dramatic.

Jaral-daridja. A lone desert oak here was a fire torch of the Wanbanbiris, for it was here they left most of their torches behind. The bulk of them were buried at the spot. The place has a single song.

Karan-karanba. The point of totemic significance here is a gap in a range of hills only a few miles from Jaral-daridja. The Wanbanbiris left more of their torches behind, and these are now gum trees. Some eucalyptus bushes mark where hare-wallaby man camped. One song belongs to the place, and refers to the discarding of the torches.

Jinja-rinja. A soakage gap in the range. Piles of boulders here represent the sleeping bodies of Jarapiri's sons, who had been carrying him. As they slept, Jarapiri slipped away from them and headed onward to Ngama; he created a short watercourse as he slithered along the ground before going beneath its surface to complete his journey. A tall bloodwood tree with a bole on one side is the transformation of the dog, Malatji, who observed Jarapiri's escape. Jinja-rinja has one song plus rich body imagery, the design of which shows Jarapiri snaking up the ritualist's back and coiling on top of his head.

Ngama, the next totemic location, is a massive rock outcrop 50 ft (15 m) high and well over 1000 ft (300 m) in length. The exact course of the approach route to it taken by Jarapiri is specifically noted by the Aborigines. The place is a major totemic site, protected by strict taboos. Its caves, cliffs, rock holes, trees, boulders, and smaller surrounding outcrops all represent members of the dreamtime group or various events that took place there in the dreamtime.

For examples, a particular cleft in the outcrop represents the vulva of a dog-woman, and a pointed rock the breast of another. A low, rocky hill to the west of the main outcrop is where Malatji and the dog-people camped, and Mountford was shown a large boulder with a flaking surface on its western end: this is the metamorphosed body of Malatji, and is a condensed source of life energy, *kurunba,* of wild dogs. During what are known as increase ceremonies, in which the fertility and fecundity of the area is perceived as being revitalized, ritualists use a small rock to flake off some of the boulder's surface to help broadcast the *kurunba* and so encourage the growth of the local wild dog population. Mountford witnessed a number of other secret rituals at Ngama, and observed the elaborate body decorations the place required. He was also shown four sacred objects – wooden boards known as *tapundas* -secreted at the site, and was allowed to take rubbings of the designs carved into them and have their meanings explained to him. There had been many more such totemic objects of wood or stone hidden away around the place, but, as with many totemic locations, most of these had been given away or sold to outsiders or tourists.

The main totemic feature at Ngama is the Jukiuta cave on the north side of the main outcrop. When Jarapiri emerged from the sandy floor of this 20-ft (6-m) deep cave after his underground journey, the dog-men of Ngama grabbed hold of him and dragged him out into the open, but they did not harm him. So, coolly, Jarapiri coiled himself up and went to sleep: he is symbolized in this pose by a large, rounded boulder at the mouth of the cave. The rest of the travelling party arrived shortly afterward, and the tracks of some of its members can be seen as distinct strata on the northern wall of the Ngama outcrop. The male members of the Jarapiri party joined forces with the Ngama dog-men and performed a major ceremony inside the cave in honour of Jarapiri, around whose stretched-out form the ceremonial activities took place. On the back wall of this cave two rather spectacular painted panels are to be seen. One is a 35-ft (11-m) long serpentine form outlined in red paint and filled in with white, which represents old Jarapiri himself. He is surrounded by small white markings indicating the dog-people of Ngama, and red horseshoe-like shapes representing camping places. Two long, closely parallel straight lines depict Jarapiri's spear. The other panel is 24 ft (7.5 m) long, with fainter, abstract images that Mountford was told referred to Jarapiri's companions. Mountford had actually visited this place in 1951, but he was then unaware that it was situated on a dreaming track. Now he observed that changes had been made to the Jarapiri panel since he had last seen it: the snake's head had been at the right end of the serpentine form in

1951, but now the head had been moved to the left end. In addition, some new images had been painted on the cave wall, while other parts of the panel had fallen into disrepair.

At Kaduna, the next totemic place after Ngama, the two groups of the Jarapiri party met up with each other. They held a great ceremony that lasted for days, after which they flopped down exhausted – various trees at the location mark their resting places.

Meanwhile, Jambali, Jarapiri's wife, together with the death-adder women, entered the ground and travelled underground to journey's end at Dada-kulanju, over 50 miles (80 km) away to the north. On stirring from their rest, the others proceeded overland along the same route. At Lililba, a gap in a range of hills a short distance on, more dancing took place, Jarapiri threw a boomerang at a passing bird, then defecated. His stool is now a solitary rock. The next site is a low, rocky hill known to the Walbiri as Minda-mindaba. Among other dreamtime events here, the Wanbanbiri men danced with what was left of their fire-torches, dropping much ash around – this is now the area of quartz pebbles to be found on the hill's otherwise bare summit. There is, or was, a strict Aboriginal prohibition against anyone eating or camping at Minda-mindaba. Jukalpi, the hare-wallaby man, left the main group and went off to camp by himself. A series of small circular rock holes today mark his camp site at Baranju-du, a depression indicates where he sat when he performed a solitary ceremony, and a rock hole over 1 ft (30 cm) deep is where he placed his sacred stone object. The main party proceeded northward, and Jukalpi rejoined them at Umbalba, a spring in Keridi Creek.

Mountford was not able to visit the final set of totemic places on the route, but his Aboriginal guides were able to give him information about them. They were mainly springs and water holes or soaks. At the final location, Dada-kulanju, Jarapiri's overland group met up with Jambali and her companions who had travelled there underground. At every place where these subterranean travellers emerged from the ground there is now a fresh-water spring.

The dreamtime travellers continued their journey northward into what Mountford described as "country about which the Ngalia and Walbiri people have no information".[3] In other words, on his dreamtime journey Jalapiri and his companions had passed the totemic boundary relating to Mountford's Aboriginal guides, beyond which they no longer knew the places or their songs, body patterns, and rituals.

●47. MALUNGU HILL to NGANGGARIDA (Haasts Bluff)

This very long dreaming track extends in a general north-west to south-east direction through Walbiri territory from a point close to the state border with Western Australia, very approximately 300 miles (480 km) north-west of Tennant Creek between Sturt Creek

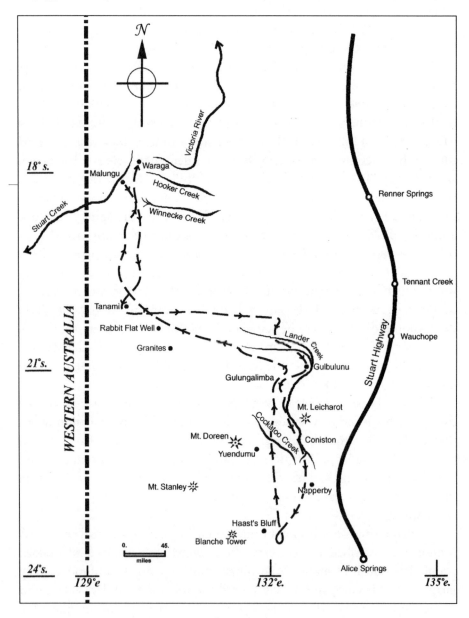

Fig. 18. Sketch map of the dreaming track of the Mamandabari men. (After M J Meggitt, 1966).

and the headwaters of the Victoria River. Malungu Hill is north-west of Winnecke Creek in the wilderness between Birrindudu Waterhole and Hooker Creek, roughly 20 miles (32 km) south-east of Inverway cattle station. (The general area is around 18°S latitude, 129° 80' E longitude.) The distance to the end point around Haasts Bluff (actually the half-way point because the dreamtime heroes return along a similar track) in the MacDonnell Ranges west of Alice Springs, is over 400 direct miles (644 km), but the actual course of the dreaming track is considerably longer.

Another anthropologist who studied the dreaming tracks in the same general area as Charles Mountford was M J Meggitt. He made a special study of *Gadjari* among the Walbiri. *Gadjari* is the the name they give to the complex of ritual, myth and song that the dreaming tracks represent. Meggitt did not field study the dreaming tracks in the way Mountford managed to do, but he drew detailed information from the three most knowledgeable elders alive in the 1950s.[4] This entry is just one of the dreaming tracks the anthropologist learned about and relates to the Mamandabari heroes, two Dreamtime beings who looked like normal men but had certain supernormal powers. The myths do not make it clear whether they were brothers or father and son. The track is described here in sketchy outline only, with extra details given here and there where the significance or nature of the track or ritual associated with it can be usefully expanded upon (Figure 18).

The Mamandabari heroes emerged from the crest of Malungu Hill, at the extreme northern boundary of what was to become Walbiri territory. Their first act was to sing their names, though what they were remains unknown. The two Dreamtime beings then looked around and decided to travel to country in the far south-east. They flew like birds from the summit of the hill down to its base, and began walking south while again singing their names. They passed the waterhole of Wurulyuwanda east of present-day Gordon Downs cattle station, and sang of the ducks and parrots they saw there. They then broke into the "distance-devouring lope of the desert men"[5] until they reached the twin waterholes of Djambugari and Djandala, where they drank and slept overnight.

The following Dreamtime day they set off again, still heading south, until they came to Djindjimirinba, the place of the firestick. Using sharp stones they fashioned two bullroarers from acacia wood and used the claw of a possum to incise a pattern into each of them. "As they do so, they sing that this pattern will represent or map the 'line' they intend to travel," Meggitt reports (Figure 19). The Mamandabari bullroarer pattern belonging to the site of Djindjimirinba, shows a part of the Mamandabari dreaming track (north is to the left). The horizontal straight lines represent the course of the dreaming

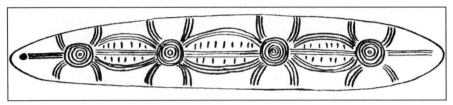

Fig. 19. The design on the bullroarer referred to in the text. The horizontal lines represent the course of part of the Mamandabari men's dreaming track (north is to the left) and the concentric circles represent the sacred sites or "big places" along that segment of the dreaming track. The arched lines represent the outswings from the main course of the route taken by the Dreamtime heroes. (After M J Meggitt)

track; the loops along it depict the outswings taken by the two Mamandabari heroes as they move off the main course of the route in order to better "create" and "mark" the country. The concentric rings represent the camps made by the heroes along the dreaming track. Left to right (that is, north to south) they are: Gadara, Walangara, Bagadji, and Wadjibili). The song was: "namba namba manda birairuwa" (literally "patterns make following these"). They then tied hairstring to the bullroarers and swung them around to test them out. After that they made digging sticks and scooped out a large oval ritual pit in the ground, singing of their activity. Next, they made two ritual poles from saplings tied with spinifex grass, and fixed them at each end of the pit, then fashioned several slender wands, which they put aside. Using chips of stone they then pierced veins in their forearms and let the blood spurt into a small hole so as to make a paste with the red earth, which they used to decorate their bodies. "Gurungu mandani gurungu wirima milidjiridjiri biwarawara gangaralududumani, " they sang ("armblood bring armblood powerful armvein decorations on top place"). They similarly decorated the ritual poles and reddened the bullroarers and the wands. They then lit the wands and, standing at each end of the pit, hurled them at each other, causing painful burns. Each of the heroes leapt into the pit in turn and "quivered in a ritually prescribed manner".[6] The quivering made particles of blood and earth fly off their bodies and fall to the ground where they transformed into amorphous spirit forms, which then merged with the features round about, thus ensuring that the essence of the Mamandabari men impregnated the locality. So it is that any woman conceiving at Djindjimirinba – or at any site marking the Mamandabari dreaming track – would give birth to a child who would be infused with Mamandabari dreaming power. After a few further ritual activities, the two Dreamtime heroes collapsed exhausted, and slept soundly.

Over the following days they continued in the general direction of what is today the community of Tanami. As they progressed, each of the heroes swung out from and back onto the main course of the track; they did this so as to see and "create" more of the country they were crossing, and they swung their bullroarers so as to "mark" the land with what became its topographical features. They proceeded in this fashion, singing of their route as they went, making camp at various places such as Bagadji Hill, Walangara waterhole, and Wadjibili rockhole. The present features of these locations were created by the actions of the Mamandabari men as they conducted various ceremonies at them. As they progressed onward from there to Tanami, they saw the smoke of an approaching bush fire, its cause unknown. Unable to outrun it, they stood their ground and quenched the flames by urinating on them. Alarmed by this close call, they hurry on to the next camp, at Gandawaranyungu, south of Tanami, and the following day pass onward through possum-dreaming country to Yulbuwanu, a dingo-dreaming place by a hill. Tired by the time they arrived there, the pair decided to jump into the air and fly eastward, crossing the line of the ibis men's dreaming track at the waterhole of Burundja. Here they learned the ceremonies of the ibis men and added them to their own repertoire. They walked on through what was to become the heartland of Walbiri country, arriving at the flood plain of Lander Creek. On the way they crossed more dreaming tracks of various other Dreamtime heroes, and as they did so the Mamandabari duo sang of these other beings and magically acquired the knowledge of their rituals.

A few more camps were made before the Mamandabari men reached Gudari soakage, which they found to their horror to be already occupied by the dangerous black *djanba* demons, who attacked them. The terrified duo escape by flying up into the air, only alighting at Liwindji soakage further down the line of their track. There they had a battle with other Dreamtime entities, but they won as their opponents were of the same nature as them, and did not possess demonic power.

The Mamandabari pair walked on to the Gulbulunu waterholes where they chanted rain-dreaming songs, causing a great storm to spring up. After sheltering from the worst of it, they set off south-west to Gulungalimba, singing of black clouds, thunder, and lightning. Later, they hungrily devoured honey from a bees' nest that they discovered in a tree, and proceeded on through an area where mulga and bloodwood trees abound, and sang of those. Over the next two nights they camped at Djaramalamala and Nganangga respectively, the big waterhole at the latter place overflowing due to the rains the Mamandabari men had invoked. Still continuing on toward Gulungalimba, the heroes grew faint from hunger and were unable to find any grass seeds to eat as they pressed on with their journey. They ultimately discovered these had been taken by an old bearded man they encountered. They berated the old fellow, who then "went underground" and travelled eastward by "dragging himself along in a sitting position".[7] This bizarre description could be a cloaked reference to the supposed ability of Clever Men to travel by means of levitation. (Aboriginal film-maker, Lorraine Maafi-Williams, claims that in the 1970s she actually witnessed an old Clever Man from Western Australia move himself forward with a curious, crippled-like motion. She could clearly see six inches of empty space between his feet and the ground surface.[8]) Interestingly, none of the Walbiri elders whom Meggitt consulted could translate the song for this episode of the Mamandabari dreaming.

After learning a circumcision ceremony from ancestral *ngarga* men at Gulungalimba, the heroes turned the course of their route back to Lander Creek and proceeded toward its southern end. They camped at various places, reaching Yulbulyu, a honeybee-dreaming site on a big hill near what became Coniston cattle station. There they ate honey to revitalize themselves before journeying on southward to the MacDonnell Ranges without further incident. When they reached the ranges east of Nganggarida (Haasts Bluff), the heroes studied the mountains, and decided they were too steep to climb and too high to fly over. So they mustered their reserves of superhuman ability and walked straight through them, creating a deep gorge. This was later to become known as Mereenie Gorge, about 300 miles (480 km) west of Alice Springs.

Beyond the mountains, the spinifex grass grew taller and denser than anywhere else on the journey, cutting the Mamandabari heroes' legs. They decided they had seen and created enough new country, and turned round to go back to their place of origin. They went north a long way underground before emerging, then continued walking, re-tracing their steps. They sang of new things they saw, and for a long way had no major incidents. But their feet were sore and their legs ached from the great journey, and they became steadily more and more exhausted. They occasionally stumbled to the ground, and the younger of the two heroes developed a profuse nose bleed. They sang of their misfortunes. Eventually, though, they neared their own country beyond Winnecke Creek and even managed to conduct a major ceremony. But unknown to them, they were being tracked by dingoes, and somewhere near Hooker Creek the pack finally attacked the weary Mamandabari men, killing them. The snarling wild dogs shook the corpses so vigorously that the heroes' hearts were tossed high in the air to fall at Waraga, where they transformed into two big rocks lying in a waterhole.

Sitting silent and unnoticed in a tree, a little budgerigar witnessed the bloody scene. Afterward, it mourned the death of the two heroes and flew off all around the country, telling people what had happened. If the bird had not done this, no one would have known about the story today, and the Walbiri elders would not have been able to tell it to the anthropologist.

COSTA RICA
Ritual and Death Paths

GUANACASTE
●48. *TILARAN-ARENAL AREA

This small Central American country is wedged between Nicaragua and Panama. The town of Tilaran is located in its north-western part, approximately 75 miles (120 km) north-west of the capital, San Jose. It can be reached by a few hours' drive along the Pan-American Highway from San Jose, taking the Tilaran turning at Canas. Tilaran is near the western end of Lake Arenal and just a few miles from its southern shore.

During the 1980s, aerial surveys (conducted by archaeologists from NASA and Colorado University using advanced imaging techniques) were made of a nationally protected archaeological zone in the mountainous rainforest around Tilaran. The earliest inhabitation of the area dates to c.9000 BC. Subsequent settlement was periodically disrupted by eruptions of Mount Arenal, the still-smouldering volcano at the eastern end of the lake. Nevertheless, after every eruption people eventually managed to re-settle the area, to a greater or lesser degree than before, and old ways of life continued much the same as ever.

Close examination of the images produced by the reconnaissance missions revealed what the investigators called "linear anomalies".[1] Subsequent intensive scrutiny of the remote-sensing data followed by ground investigation and excavations revealed that these lines (some still visible as depressions in the ground) were traces of footpaths dating from the "Silencio Phase" (c.AD 500–1200). Some of them related to a large Silencio Phase cemetery identified on the archaeologists' maps as site "G-150" in a watershed area on the Continental Divide about 4 miles (6.5 km) due east of Tilaran. The aerial photographs also showed segments of linear traces extending through much of the country between the cemetery and Tilaran, though most of these were not investigated on the ground.

The prehistoric footpaths were originally quite narrow – one or two feet (30-60 cm) wide – but rain erosion over the centuries had made their traces wider in some places. These routes had been intensively walked and were very direct, though on steep inclines there were side-loops leading off the main course of the path to minimize gradients. These secondary paths had presumably been for the infirm or those carrying particularly heavy loads only, as they had been used much less than the well-worn paths "going straight up and down slopes". "The routing decisions for these paths were quite different from those used for routing of contemporary roads, of cattle paths, other animal paths, or other recent and historic features, " the investigating archaeologists emphasized. They continued:

> In contrast, these prehistoric paths follow relatively straight lines
> . . . hills have paths travelling over their tops rather than around
> their bottoms, and valleys have paths directly descending to their
> low points and directly ascending to the other sides rather than
> contouring around toward their headwaters . . . In one case, a
> short path from a village to a cemetery went right over the top
> of a small hill rather than around it.[2]

Special routes, then, but what were they for? It turns out that their purpose was uncannily close to that of Old World death roads – they had been trod for the carrying of corpses, and, also, to collect laja, a volcanic stone used for tombs. The multiple paths leading from the Silencio cemetery "point in various directions toward villages that buried their dead in that cemetery". Paths also led out southward from the cemetery to a spring; these paths had been particularly heavily used suggesting ritual activity rather than the straightforward conveyance of the dead or funerary material. Within the cemetery, archaeological evidence was uncovered of cooking utensils, stone tools, and occupational rubbish, showing that people stayed there for long periods. The archaeologists pictured extensive ritual activity taking place in the cemetery, with the heavy traffic to and from the spring being an integral part of this. The experts surmised that the rituals would have been directed toward the ancestral spirits.

MEXICO
Sacred Roads

QUINTANA ROO
●49. COBÁ to YAXUNÁ

Cobá is situated in the north-eastern sector of the Yucatan Peninsula, in northern Quintana Roo. It is on a road that runs south to Tulum from Nuevo Xcan on highway 180 (which links Merida in the west to Cancun on the east coast of the peninsula). The road south is followed for just under 28 miles (45 km) then a right turn is taken onto a road that shortly leads to the parking area at Cobá. Another route, if coming directly from Cancun, is south along coastal highway 307 for 81 miles (130 km) turning right to Cobá (and Nuevo Xcan) just before reaching Tulum. This road is followed for approximately 27 miles (43.5 km) then a left turn is taken into the Cobá complex. Cobá is a fairly remote and isolated jungle site so it is worth knowing that there is a hotel and restaurant there, plus a few small restaurants nearby. Cobá is a large, sprawling complex, and it is a good idea to hire one of the Mayan guides who wait around the main entrance to the complex off the parking area. A good site map is essential. Yaxuná, a relatively minor archaeological site, lies some 60 miles (96.5 km) west of Cobá across the Quintana Roo state line in Yucatan. It is situated about 13 miles (21 km) south of Chichen Itza, which is on Highway 180, and can be accessed via country roads.

Cobá is a vast complex of Mayan temples (including pyramid temples), stelae, plazas, public buildings, and other structures built among and around a set of small lakes, the main ones being Lake Cobá and Lake Macanxoc. Many of the sites that comprise this site have yet to be examined archaeologically. The various main centres or building groups within the complex are scattered throughout the rainforest and are connected by poorly signposted modern tracks. It is difficult to appreciate now that Cobá was a great centre during the middle and later parts of the Mayan Classic era (CAD 600–900) and its origins were even earlier. At its height Cobá supported an estimated population of 55, 000 over an area of 27 square miles (65 sq km).

Cobá is the best place to visit if seeking examples of the mysterious Mayan causeways or *sacbeob,* as approximately fifty examples have been uncovered there to date, more than at any other Mayan site. These causeways ranged from 9–60 ft (3–18 m) in width and not only connected buildings within the Cobá complex but also extended to far-flung sites and even to distant Mayan cities.

We know little about the spectral or mythic *sacbeob* (see Chapter Four) or what they connected within or beyond the complex, except that surviving local

Mayan lore states that an aerial route in the form of an invisible blood-filled tube ran from near Tulum on the east coast, through part of the Cobá complex and on to former Mayan cities, now occupied by the present-day towns of Valladolid and Merida – a total distance of some 300 miles (480 km).[1]

The great pyramid temple of Nohoch Mul in Cobá is a major centre for physical causeways. Its summit rises over 100 ft (30 m) so that it projects above the rainforest canopy (Plate 63). Running west from this pyramid is the longest Mayan causeway that has yet been identified: it extends for 62 miles (100 km) in a virtually dead straight line to the ancient Mayan centre of Yaxuná. The explorer Thomas Gann happened across a segment of it in the 1920s. He described what he saw as "a great elevated road, or causeway 32 ft (10 m) wide ... the sides were built of great blocks of cut stone, many weighing

Plate 63. The Nohoch Mul pyramid at Cobá, Quintana Roo, Mexico, rising amid the steam coming off the rainforest. This site is a major node for several Mayan causeways or sacbeob, including the one that connects with Yaxuná.

hundreds of pounds ... it ran, as far as we followed it, straight as an arrow, and almost flat as a rule".[2] The typical structure of the causeway consisted of retaining walls filled with rubble, topped with concreted cobbles and then surfaced with a form of stucco.

Parts of the basic structure of this causeway to Yaxuná are visible here and there within the Cobá complex near Nohoch Mul, but the feature is soon lost in the surrounding jungle. Nevertheless, archaeologists have mapped it all the way to Yaxuná; *en route* it crosses Highway 295, which runs from the north coast down through Valladolid and on southward – it is worth accessing the causeway off this road to gain an idea of the deep-jungle state of the feature. The *sacbe* intersects the highway at right-angles 1¾ miles (22 km) south of Valladolid and a little over a mile (1.5 km) south of a small place called Tixcacalcupul. The exact point is marked by a somewhat battered road signs saying "Camino Maya". The causeway is best accessed from the east side of the road; it is necessary to go a short distance into trees and undergrowth but eventually tumbled white stones will be seen (Plate 64). Here, 38 miles (61 km) west of Cobá, the great causeway is now in a ruinous state, as it is for most of its length.

Plate 64. This jumble of stones deep in the jungle is all that now marks the course of the Cobá-Yaxuná causeway for much of its length.

YUCATAN
●50. KABAH

Highway 261 cuts through the ruins of this complex. The road runs about 38 miles (61 km) south from the city of Merida via Uman and Muna to the major archaeological site of Uxmal where it bears east, then on for about a further 13 miles (21 km) through Santa Elena (where it bears south again) to Kabah.

There are numerous temples and other major buildings on both sides of the road, some of those on the east side being exceptional examples of versions of the mid-to-late Classic era (*c.*AD 700–1000) Puuc Style Mayan architecture. ("Puuc Style" refers to a specialized mosaic technique involving the fixing of ornate lattice-like façades containing masks and other designs

Plate 65. The course of the causeway or sacbe that once connected the Mayan ceremonial centres of Uxmal and Kabah is preserved by this grass strip where it approached the Kabah Arch.

to existing, plainer structures.) In particular, the site is famed for the Codz-Poop building, also known as the Palace of the Masks for the very good reason that its

Plate 66. Part of the south façade of the Palace at Sayil, Yucatan, Mexico.

exterior is covered with an overpowering plethora of mask designs, specifically those of the rain-god, Chac, with his elephant trunk-like nose or snout.

The main point of interest for the seeker of roads-less-travelled here at Kabah, though, is the so-called "Arch" on the other, western, side of Highway 261. This tall, plain structure seems always to have been freestanding. It is located on a stepped platform or ramp, and spans 14 ft (4.3 m). It is believed to have formed the gateway to Kabah, or at least to its ceremonial core, and stands at one end of a 15-ft (4.6-m) wide *sacbe* that connected with the great Mayan centre of Uxmal approximately 10 miles (16 km) to the north. Extending north from the Kabah Arch today, an indication of the course of this once-paved *sacbe* is preserved as a grassy strip (Plate 65).

●51.SAYIL

This is about 5 miles (8 km) from Kabah. Highway 261 is followed south from Kabah for about 2½ miles before branching left onto a side road (the so-called "Puuc Highway") ultimately leading to Oxkutzcab via Cooperativa. Sayil is a short distance along this road, on the right.

The first thing that impresses the visitor to this site is the huge Palace, one of the masterpieces of Mayan architecture (Plate 66). Over 230 ft (71 m) in length, it stands three terraced storeys high and has ninety-four rooms. The middle storey is punctuated by entrance columns. The building was constructed in various stages between *c.*AD 700 and 1000. As with Kabah, Sayil is a Puuc-style complex, but here the decorative mosaics tend to be controlled additions to the main structures.

Plate 67. The course of the former causeway or sacbe at Sayil.

The Palace looks out over a plaza, and on the far side of it from the Palace the preserved dead-straight course of a *sacbe* leads off southward into the trees (Plate 67). After about a quarter of a mile (400 m) this reaches a ruined temple on a small pyramidal base known as the Mirador. The ruins of other temples and buildings are hidden away amongst the trees: extensions of the *sacbe* lead on to some of them, while it is necessary to take side trails off the sacred route to reach the others. Some of these structures are growing back into the forest, creating a strongly romantic impression of lost civilisations.

ZACATECAS
●52. LA QUEMADA (CHICOMOZTOC)

The archaeological site of La Quemada, also known as Chicomoztoc, lies about 30 miles (48 km) south of Zacatecas, a fairly isolated but beautiful Spanish Colonial city situated at an altitude of over 8,000 feet (2, 440 m) in northern Mexico some 300 miles (480 km) north-west of Mexico City. The lonely ruins of La Quemada can be accessed by means of a 5½-mile (9-km) long minor road leading eastward off Highway 54 (which runs south from Zacatecas to Guadalajara). The ruins are closed to visitors on Mondays, and there is no entrance fee on Sundays. Zacatecas has a small airport handling internal flights, including a few from Mexico City.

The ruins of La Quemada are as enigmatic as they are spectacular. They are focused on a solitary and dramatic rocky hill or ridge that is crowned by two peaks. Approaching from the south, the visitor passes a now-roofless building within which stand eleven massive columns. No one knows the function of this "Hall of Columns", but in March each year, around the spring equinox, the Huichol Indians – a most ancient people – come from their homeland in the east to hold a secret ceremony within the building using the hallucinogenic cactus, peyote, which is sacramental to them. They seem to shun La Quemada at other times. An enormous stone stairway leads up the lower part of the eastern side of the rocky hill from a precinct containing a mysterious flat-topped pyramid (Plate 68). From the top of this broad stairway paths wind around the rocks, leading past the ruins of temples, shrines and ceremonial platforms and plazas built onto terraces cut into the hillside. While the citadel-like nature of the site seems apparent, the ceremonial and ritual structures it contains make it clear that religious activities took place there.

La Quemada is thought to have belonged to a little-known ancient people referred to by scholars as the Chakhihuites and to have reached its heyday between *c.*AD 600 and 800. It was finally destroyed by fire, during either an attack from outside or an insurrection from within.

Plate 68. The truncated pyramid and part of the citadel at la Quemada, Zacatecas, Mexico.

The broad, flat landscape surrounding La Quemada is punctuated by occasional isolated hills or ridges. It is criss-crossed by the remnants of many straight causeways often extending for miles. Their construction consisted of low, parallel retaining walls built on top of the ground, the space between them being filled level with rubble and then surfaced with paving. (It is thought that there were also some routes that consisted of nothing more than straight pathways of uniform width made from packed earth.) The first documented account made of them was by a British engineer, G F Lyon, in 1826. He described the causeways he examined as being from 12–45 ft (3.7–13.8 m) wide and "perfectly straight", crossing rivers, hillsides and ridges as well as flat open land. They ran to caves in cliffs and distant peaks, and interlinked ceremonial structures such as temples, pyramids, and plazas.

Modern surveys conducted by Charles Trombold of Washington University, St Louis, have confirmed the existence of over 100 miles (160 km) of causeways in the region. Some of them converge onto (or diverge from) the citadel, and others connect with outlying sites or natural features.

Platforms, ramps, ceremonial stairs, sunken courts, and altars were placed on the causeways or at their ends. Because the landscape was so easy for walking the causeways were unlikely to be intended for normal foot traffic. There is also no specific evidence to show a military use for them, but like most formal roads in the ancient Americas they could have been multi-functional. "Almost certainly they . . . were associated with ritual activities," Trombold concludes. He points out that they represent "the tip of a cultural iceberg in that behind their presence lies extensive planning, engineering, mobilization of labour and monumental-scale construction".[3]

The roads are now, at best, difficult to see and are often invisible to the casual observer. One of the better vantage points is a major plaza high up on the southern end of the citadel, which affords extensive views to the south and west. From there, the courses of a few causeways can be discerned by the existence of linear stretches of vegetation (Plate 69). Two particularly broad causeways approached La Quemada directly from the south, cutting through what is now an area of nopal cacti near the foot of the southern edge of the citadel: their courses can just be discerned as faint brownish lines amid the dark green of the cacti.

Plate 69. The author looks out over the landscape from high up on the La Quemada citadel. The diagonal line of vegetation on the right marks the course of one of the mysterious straight causeways around the site. There are also others embedded in the cactus plantation behind the author. (Sol Devereux)

UNITED STATES OF AMERICA
Shamanic and Ritual Routes

CALIFORNIA
●53. DEATH VALLEY

The valley is situated in south-east California alongside the Nevada state line. Las Vegas is 100 miles (160 km) to the east, Fresno 150 miles (240 km) to the west, with not a great deal of major habitation in between. Barstow is 100 miles (160 km) to the south; the best way into the valley from this direction is via Interstate 15 running north-east from Barlow, then via State Highway 127 north off that. If after 58 miles (93 km) Highway 178 is taken west off this (just past Shoshone), then Death Valley is entered at its south end after about 20 miles (32 km) – Highway 178 can then be followed north through the valley. Alternatively, Highway 190 can be taken west off Highway 127 some 21 miles (33.5 km) further north at Death Valley Junction, and this leads directly past Zabriskie Point into the heart of the valley. From the west, various roads lead east off Highway 395 between China Lake and Lone Pine – the best being Highway 190, which crosses the Panamint Valley and reaches Death Valley in approximately 70 miles (112 km). When visiting Death Valley and its region drivers should ensure that their vehicle is in good working order and fully-fuelled, and carry ample spare water both for the radiator and for drinking. There are a few paved roads through the valley but others are merely surfaced with gravel. A four-wheel drive vehicle is advisable though not strictly essential. For walking in Death Valley, thick-soled boots are essential, as is a map, and a compass or GPS device (a hand-held electronic device used to fix a position by triangulating on orbiting satellites) can be useful. The use of a broad-brimmed hat, sunglasses and high-factor sun cream is strongly advised and, because of the sun's intensity, it is sensible to keep most of the skin covered by clothing. Few places in the valley offer accommodation (so advance booking is advised). Furnace Creek and Stovepipe Wells are the main ones, and also provide fuel and basic supplies and include ranger stations.

Death Valley is oriented roughly north-south. It is almost 100 miles (160 km) long and 25 miles (40 km) wide, and its floor reaches down nearly 300 ft (90 m) below sea level. It is one of the world's hottest places – a temperature of 57 °C (134 °F) was once recorded there. The convoluted and amazingly colourful strata of this "wasteland in the middle of nowhere"[1] reveal its tortured two billion years of geological history.

Tens of thousands of years ago a deep lake occupied the valley; when this eventually dried out other, lesser lakes came and went, a sequence that came to a close when the area lost its battle against encroaching aridity. It was this succession of ancient lakes that left the salt pans and dried-mud "playas" that now share the valley floor with areas of scrub and sand dunes.

People inhabited Death Valley from 7000–6000 BC, when a cool period allowed the last, shallow lake to occupy part of the valley floor, but this dried up about two thousand years ago as hotter, arid conditions finally prevailed. Along with Panamint Valley to the east and the land extending to Charleston Peak outside Las Vegas to the west, Death Valley was known to the Shoshone as part of *tiwiniyarivipi* – "where the stories begin and end" or "mythic land, sacred country".[2]

Unknown to most visitors today, Death Valley (and Panamint Valley) has mysterious ground markings and other features left by ancient American Indians at various remote and obscure locations within it. These features can range from straggling lines of small rock cobbles pressed into the ground, to patterns incised into the hard, brittle desert pavement revealing the lighter subsurface, to small shrines and vision-quest areas built from pebbles or larger rocks. What were all these for? Archaeologist Jay von Werlhof suggests they were a form of weather magic: he envisages the shamans of ancient Indian groups in Death Valley struggling to put a brake on the increasingly arid conditions. "Attempting to rearrange forces . . . was part of the shaman's way, " he points out. "The symbols employed in earthen art, as well as the act of placing them conspicuously on the earth, seemingly reflect an enormous effort to induce rejuvenation of a dying ecosystem."[3] It may seem strange to us today that the laying out of ground markings and subtle structures should be seen as a magical act, but it is known that the Yuman Indians to the southeast of this region, in Arizona, did indeed make marks on the ground as part of their exercise of supernatural power.

One of Death Valley's secreted sacred sites is situated on a low volcanic hillock south of Furnace Creek (in the centre of the valley) in the vicinity of the salt pan known as the Devil's Golf Course.[4] It is small and isolated, rather like an island, with its summit below sea level – just one example of the strangeness of Death Valley. It has a cover of dark volcanic rocks and pebbles, lightly cemented onto the subsurface by natural action. Cutting through this is the clean swathe of a path formed by the careful and precise removal of some of this rock debris in ancient times (Plates 70 and 71). Although the path traverses the whole hill, it comes from nowhere and goes to no destination in the surrounding terrain. It belongs just to the hill, and is a sacred or ritual path. This is indicated by the fact that the path passes through or by the remains of various ritual features, including three stone mounds in a cleared area forming a shrine or sacred enclosure (Plate 72). Where the path enters and exits the cleared area small arrangements of stone are laid out like

Plates 70 and 71. Two views of the ritual path in Death Valley.

Plate 72. *The remains of the shrine site that the Death Valley ritual path leads to and through. The original cairn of stones has been much reduced, but note the cleared area around it and the lines of small rocks radiating out from it. Ancient sacred sites in Death Valley are subtle places.*

symbolic little gates, interpreted by archaeologists as "spirit breaks" to protect the shrine area from any unwanted supernatural influences passing along the path. Also in the complex are vision-quest sites, and scatters of quartz. This rock was vitally important for ceremonial purposes because the Indians could strike it to produce "magic fire" – quartz produces an electrical discharge and a flash of light when it is struck by another piece of quartz, an effect known as "triboluminescence". This effect was widely used by many other ancient American Indians, the Maya being another example.

Jay von Werlhof comments that to the Indian mind certain trails or paths had power: "While geoglyphs (ground markings) and trails did have separate particular roles, generically they fulfilled similar spiritual purposes."[5]

COLORADO
●54. LOWRY RUINS

This site is situated in the extreme south-western corner of the state in the region known as the "Four Corners", where the modern states of Colorado, Utah, Arizona and New Mexico meet. The main town nearest to the ruins is Cortez. From here, Highway

666 is taken northward for 18 miles (29 km) through Lewis and Yellow Jacket to Pleasant Point, where a road (partly unpaved) leads off west (left) to Lowry Ruins about 9 miles (14.5 km) distant.

The Anasazi survived as an identifiable culture for about a thousand years before disappearing c.AD 1400 for reasons unknown – though drought coupled with religious friction could well have been involved. They were a collection of related cultural groups and were accomplished builders, engineers, astronomers, and traders. They variously had a number of major and countless minor centres throughout the San Juan Basin, which spreads for about 400 miles (644 km) across the "Four Corners" region. Some of the major centres included Mesa Verde in this state, and Aztec and Chaco Canyon (see the following entry) in New Mexico, and though the Lowry site does not measure up to these it was nevertheless important, as evidenced by its Great Kiva, one of the largest in the region. Kivas were semi-subterranean ceremonial and ritual chambers, and extra large "great" ones obviously indicated a place of special significance. Main Anasazi pueblos were first and foremost religious centres, no matter what other, more mundane or secular functions they had.

The Lowry Pueblo was built c.AD 1060 on top of an eighth-century settlement. To the south lies the long ridge of Ute Mountain, venerated to this day by the Ute Indians who see in its form the figure of a sleeping chieftain. At its height, Lowry Pueblo boasted forty rooms, some standing three stories high, and eight small kivas in addition to the Great Kiva, which was used throughout the time the place was inhabited. One of the small kivas, inside the pueblo structure, had been painted, and some of this decoration has survived. The pueblo was abandoned sometime after AD 1200 for unknown reasons.

There is some archaeological evidence that parts of the pueblo were not used for everyday activities, as though a section of it was set aside for religious/ceremonial purposes. Indeed, it may have been a pilgrimage place because the Great Kiva had one of the mysterious, straight Anasazi ceremonial roads running to it. This may have been part of a system extending from Chaco Canyon (see following entry), for archaeologists detect a Chacoan influence at the Lowry Pueblo. Little is to be seen of this sacred route now, but fieldwork for this Sampler was carried out in May, the time of year when the arid landscape blooms, and near the kiva the course of the road was partially revealed because purple desert flowers were growing along it, presumably preferring the softer ground covering the road's foundation; a purple road of the Anasazi, the Ancient Ones, leading to one of their sacred places.

NEW MEXICO
●55. CHACO CANYON

The canyon is situated in the north-west corner of New Mexico, roughly 100 miles (160 km) north-west of Albuquerque and 50 miles (80 km) south of Farmington. It is an isolated, remote place and ultimately it is necessary to use unpaved roads to reach it. For that reason, weather conditions should be checked before setting out for the canyon; a four-wheel drive vehicle is advisable although a two-wheel drive car will suffice in dry conditions. The canyon can be approached from various directions. From Albuquerque, Interstate 25 is taken north for 16 miles (25.5 km) at which point State Highway 44 is taken on the left (north-west) past Bernalillo. This is followed for approximately 100 miles (160 km) before taking a left turn (south-west) onto Route 7950 (perhaps marked 7900 or 57 at the turn) just before Nageezi is reached. This road leads to Chaco Canyon about 20 miles (32 km) away. At first paved, it soon becomes a broad, dirt track. From Farmington, Highway 64 is taken east 13 miles (21 km) as far as Bloomington, then Highway 44 south (right) to just beyond Nageezi, where a right-hand turn is made onto the road leading to Chaco Canyon. From the south, Interstate 40 is taken east from Gallup as far as Thoreau, where a left turn (north) is taken onto Route 605. Shortly after Crownpoint on this road a right-hand (east) turn is made onto Route 9 toward White Horse. Further along this, unpaved Route 57 on the left (north) is taken to the canyon. There is only camping accommodation at Chaco Canyon, but it has an excellent Visitor Centre with basic facilities in addition to a museum, bookshop, video theatre and ranger information.

This broad, shallow canyon cutting east-west through high desert country appears to have been a key ritual centre for one major group of Anasazi. It seems people came to Chaco Canyon at certain times in the year for whatever purpose, then returned to their scattered communities around and about, leaving just a caretaker staff behind to tend the ceremonial buildings there and carry out craft work. These structures are now referred to as "Great Houses". One of them, Pueblo Bonito, is the largest prehistoric ruin in the United States and some commentators have interpreted it as being the largest apartment block in the US, prior to the nineteenth century. However, the investigating archaeologists who excavated it found its many rooms bare, providing little evidence of continuous habitation.

As the centre of a system of ancient ceremonial roads, Chaco Canyon is the most significant place in the south-western United States for treaders of old and forgotten sacred ways to visit. These Chacoan roads are in the main distinctly straight, and converge on (or diverge from) the canyon (Figure 20). They are engineered features over 30 ft wide (9 m) wide, a curious fact considering that the Anasazi used neither wheeled vehicles nor beasts of burden. It is even more

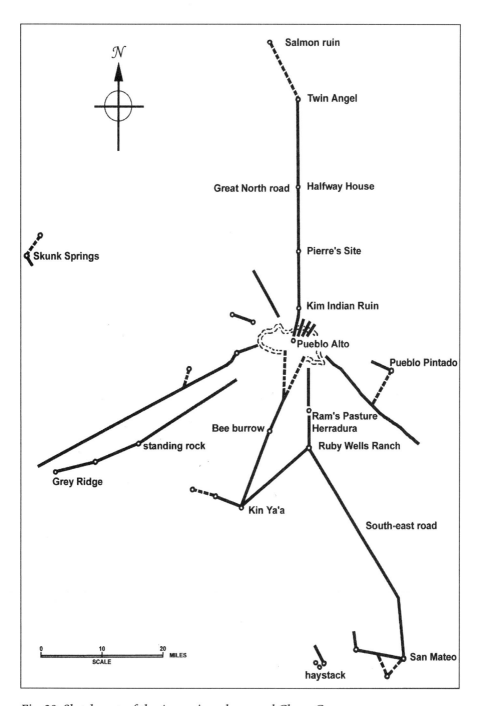

Fig. 20. Sketch map of the Anasazi roads around Chaco Canyon.

curious, because NASA aerial infrared photography has further revealed that some sections of roads have up to two parallel sections, like modern multi-lane highways. The roads link not only the Great Houses within the canyon but also others scattered across the surrounding arid country. Great House architecture was seemingly designed to accommodate the roads, because gates in the walls allowed the roads to pass through, and in some cases rooms in the building had no internal access but opened out only onto the roads. Some of the roads are known to extend for tens of miles, and perhaps much further because traces of Anasazi roads have been uncovered not only in southern New Mexico, far from Chaco Canyon, but also in the contiguous states of Utah, Arizona and Colorado (note previous entry). The roads connect to the edge, the rimrock, of Chaco Canyon and steep, broad rock-hewn stairways lead down the canyon walls from them, though most of these stone steps are now eroded to virtual invisibility (Plate 73).

It is suspected by some archaeologists that the Chacoan road system may have linked the Great Kivas in the more important Anasazi centres scattered

Plate 73. An example of one of the eroded stone staircases in Chaco Canyon. These rock-hewn stairs connected with the enigmatic "roads" surrounding the canyon.

across the San Juan Basin. In 1988, for instance, one hour of aerial reconnaissance during low-angle sunlight revealed 6 miles (10 km) of Anasazi road fragments near Bluff, in south-eastern Utah. "Directly associated with this road were two previously known Great Kiva/Great House sites . . . and an isolated Great Kiva, " the investigators reported.[6] Subsequent ground investigation led to more road segment discoveries. If there was this interrelated Anasazi road system, then it would have been a supreme geographical expression of ceremonial, or, probably more precisely, ritual activity, on a par with the dreaming tracks of the Australian Aborigines.

It may well have been that in keeping with many similar ancient American features these special roads served multiple purposes, including mundane transport, but there can be no doubt that religious activity was one of them. Animal sculptures and shrines have been found on some of the roads, and scatters of pottery found along them indicate ritual ceramic breakage, a common practice in many cultures of antiquity. That the roads were special is further evidenced by the fact that they were obviously deliberately engineered when simple trackways would have served secular purposes just as well. Thomas Sever, a NASA archaeologist who has made a special study of the features, additionally points out that the most common feature of the Chaco roads "is their straight line course which is maintained in spite of topographic obstacles". The reason for this, he admits, "is not entirely clear and has never been satisfactorily answered."[7] It will be recalled that in Chapter One the late John Hyslop was cited as remarking that ancient roads constructed in extraordinary ways "may reflect ritual or symbolic concerns" and that solely materialistic interpretations of such special Native American roads "are bound to fail". These comments are well directed toward the Chacoan roads. Significantly, Navajo elder, Hosteen Beyal, told an investigating archaeologist in the 1920s that the Chacoan features "were not really roads" although they may look like them.[8] The archaeologist in question, Neil Judd, later had conversations with other Navajo elders; he never revealed the nature of those discussions, but he subsequently began referring to the roads as "ceremonial highways".[9]

Attempting to see the thousand-year-old roads on the ground in and around Chaco Canyon is a difficult task because the effects of time, weather, and human activity have almost erased their traces. Until one's eye becomes trained, it is hard to discern the subtle linear depressions (called "swales") that signal the presence of Chacoan roads, even when looking directly at one of them. Probably the best place to try is Pueblo Alto, a Great House on the northern rimrock of the canyon. It can be accessed by means of a steep rock tunnel leading up through the north wall of the canyon behind the Great House called Kin Kletso, a short distance to the west of Pueblo Bonito. This natural tunnel opens out onto the flat rimrock surface, which is then traversed to the north until the ruins of Pueblo Alto appear. A notice board at the site depicts a bird's eye view of the several roads that lead to or from the place. In particular there is the major north-south route that archaeologists have dubbed the "Great North Road" (as an oblique reference to the major Roman road that runs north from London). Standing beside the ruined walls of Pueblo Alto affords a magnificent view northward across the desert toward mountain peaks almost 100 miles (160 km) away. With careful observation, the course of the Great North Road can just be made out as it cuts down to the white sands of a (usually) dry river bed a short distance to the north. A useful tip for trying to observe these ancient and mysterious roads is to wait until just before sunset: as the sun sinks low over the western horizon, the shallow depressions marking their courses increasingly reveal themselves as soft and patchy shadowy lines running though the desert. For fleeting moments the Otherworld enigma that the roads represent flickers faintly into visibility. (For safety's sake, it is important to get back down quickly onto the canyon floor before darkness descends.)

In order to access Pueblo Alto from Kim Kletso it is necessary to register for a "Backcountry Use Permit". This is intended as a safety measure. The permit is issued by the site rangers at the Visitor Centre. Make sure to obtain a map of the canyon at the same time as registering for the permit. Also, the extremely helpful rangers can suggest where to go to glimpse the more substantial remnants of road segments, as well as indicating where rock-hewn stairways are still visible along the canyon walls.

To visit Chaco Canyon seeking signs of its ancient roads helps one to more keenly appreciate the mystery of ancient Otherworld routes, to understand that in former times people lived within a different geography to ourselves. In some regards, perhaps, they knew their way round better than we do today.

REFERENCES AND NOTES

(i) Dates given immediately after certain book titles denote original publication.

(ii) Numbers given in parenthesis at the end of some entries indicate specific page numbers.

PART ONE

Introduction

1. This whole complex area is discussed in depth in Paul Devereux's *Haunted Land*, Piatkus, London, 2001.

Chapter One

1. Chatwin, Bruce, *The Songlines*, Viking, Markham, Ontario, 1987.

2. Kahn, Miriam, "Your Place and Mine: Sharing Emotional Landscapes in Wamira, Papua New Guinea", in Feld, S., and Basso, K. (eds.), *Senses of Place*, School of American Research Press, Santa Fe, 1996.

3. Helen Watson cited in Turnbull, David, *Maps Are Territories*, (1989), University of Chicago Press, Chicago, 1993. (28)

4. Cited in Campbell, Joseph, *Historical Atlas of World Mythology, Part 2: Mythologies of the Great Hunt*, Harper and Row, New York, 1988. (136-7)

5. Cowan, James, *The Mysteries of the Dream-Time*, Prism Press, Bridport, 1989.

6. Chatwin, 1987, op.cit.; Snyder, Gary, *The Practice of the Wild*, North Point Press, San Francisco, 1990.

7. Helen Watson cited in Turnbull, 1989/1993, op.cit. (30-31)

8. David Lewis cited in ibid. (53-3)

9. Chatwin, 1987, op. cit. (108)

10. Elkin, A.P., *Aboriginal Men of High Degree*, (1977), Inner Traditions, Rochester, Vermont, 1994. (62-3)

11. Ibid. (64)

Chapter Two

1. Jackson, Nigel, "Dead On", in *The Ley Hunter*, no.119, 1993. (24)

2. Harte, Jeremy, "Show me the Way to Go Home", in *3rd Stone*, April-June, 1998.

3. Haslam, W., cited in Langdon, Arthur, *Old Cornish Crosses*, Joseph Pollard, Truro, 1896. (7)

4. Ginzburg, Carlo, *Ecstasies – Deciphering the Witches' Sabbath*, (1989), Penguin Books, London, 1992. (5)

5. Hinze, Christe, and Diederich, Ulf, *Ostpreussiche Sagen*, Eugen Diederich,

Munich, 1991. (Cited in Magin, Ulrich, "The Flightpath of the Corpses", *The Ley Hunter,* no.131, 1999.)

6. *Handwortbuch de deutschen Aberglaubens,* de Gruyters, 1933. (Translated by Ulrich Magin in *The Ley Hunter,* no. 116, 1992.)

7. Evans Wentz, Y.W., *The Fairy-Faith in Celtic Countries,* (1911), Colin Smythe, Gerrards Cross, 1977.(218)

8. Saward, Jeff, "The labyrinth as spirit trap", in *The Ley Hunter,* no.133, 1998.

9. Evans, E. Estyn, *Irish Folk Ways,* Routledge & Kegan Paul, London, 1957. (293)

10. Caciola, Nancy, "Wraiths, Revenants and Ritual in Medieval Culture", in *Past and Present,* no. 152, 1996.

11. Palmer, John, "Notes on church and corpse roads in Holland", in *The Ley Hunter,* no.127, 1997.

12. Caciola, Nancy, "Spirits seeking bodies: death, possession and communal memory in the Middle Ages", in Gordon, Bruce, and Marshall, Peter, (eds.), *The Place of the Dead,* Cambridge University Press, Cambridge, 2000. (66)

13. Gordon, Bruce, "Malevolent ghosts and ministering angels: apparitions and pastoral care in the Swiss Reformation", in ibid. (93)

14. Menefee, Samuel Pyeatt, "Dead Reckoning: the Church Porch Watch in British Society", in Davidson, Hilda Ellis, (ed.), *The Seer,* John Donald, Edinburgh, 1989.

15. Palmer, John, "The Folklore of Death: The Precursors", and "The Precursors III", *The Ley Hunter,* no. 129, 1998.

16. Evans Wentz, 1911/1977, op. cit. (213-5)

17. Thomas, W. Jenkyn, *The Welsh Fairy Book,* (1907), University of Wales Press, Cardiff, 1995.

18. Ibid.

19. Simpson, Jacqueline, *Icelandic Folktales and Legends,* University of California Press, Berkeley, 1972. (176-8)

20. Puhvel, Martin, *The Crossroads in Folklore and Myth,* American University Studies, Peter Lang, New York, 1989.

21. Rees, Alwyn and Brinley, *Celtic Heritage,* Thames & Hudson, London, 1961. (94)

22. Davies, Jonathan Caredig, *Folk-Lore of West and Mid-Wales,* (1911), Llanerch, Lampeter, 1992.(149-50)

23. See Ginzburg, Carlo, *Ecstasies – Deciphering the Witches' Sabbath,* (1989), Penguin Books, London, 1992, and also Pocs, Eva, *Between the Living and the Dead,* (1977), Central European University Press, Budapest, 1999.

24. The whole matter is teased out further in Paul Devereux's *Haunted Land,* Piatkus, London, 2001.

Chapter Three

1. Sivier, David, "The Limners of Faerie", in *Magonia,* no.71, 2000.

2. It could be that some of these fairy lights are a little-known natural phenomenon: Cornwall has much geological faulting and is rich in minerals, and it is thought that unusual light phenomena can be generated over such terrain. In fact, Cornwall is known to produce such lights at times of earthquakes. In the week leading up to an earthquake in 1996, for instance, there were numerous reports of strange lights being seen in the Cornish skies. The British Geological Survey carried out a study of these reports to add to their archives containing similar accounts from the region going back a century or more.

3. Mac Manus, Dermot, *The Middle Kingdom* (1959), Colin Smythe, Gerrards Cross, 1979.

4. Keightley, Thomas, *The Fairy Mythology,* (1892), Wildwood House, London, 1981. (299)

5. Ben Jonson, *Masque of Oberon.*

6. Bottrell, William. *Traditions and Hearthside Stories of West Cornwall,* (1870-80), Llanerch (abridged edition), 1989. (84)

7. Some argue that in the Irish case the term derives from the Gaelic for a goat, *Puc,* but it could be that the goat got its name from the old land spirit!

8. Wilby, Emma, "The Witch's Familiar and the Fairy in Early Modern England and Scotland", in *Folklore,* no.111, 2000.

9. Briggs, Katherine, *The Anatomy of Puck,* Routledge and Kegan Paul, London, 1959. (99)

10. Mac Manus, Dermot, *The Middle Kingdom,* (1959), Colin Smythe, Gerrards Cross, 1973. (44-5)

11. Sacred tree traditions occur all over the world, of course, not only in Ireland. In England, the finding of a Neolithic timber circle enclosing the upturned bole of a huge, ancient tree on the coast of Norfolk in 1999 revealed just how far back the veneration of trees went in this part of the world. See Paul Devereux's *The Sacred Place,* Cassell, London, 2000, for further discussion and illustration of sacred trees.

12. Harte, "Hidden Laughter: The Dorset Fairy Tradition", *3rd Stone,* no. 29, 1998.

13. Leger-Gordon, Ruth E., *The Witchcraft and Folklore of Dartmoor,* EP Publishing, East Ardsley, 1973. (21)

14. Signy, Larry, "Mystery of the Mound", in *The Farnborough News, 2* March, 1990.

15. Kirk, Robert, *The Secret Commonwealth of Elves, Fauns, & Fairies,* (1691), Helios, Toddington, 1964. (4)

16. Edmund Jones, 1779, cited in Olding, Frank, "Fairy Lore in 18th-century Monmouthshire", in *3rd Stone,* no.31, 1998. (20)

17. Evans Wentz, Y.W., *The Fairy-Faith in Celtic Countries,* (1911), Colin Smythe, Gerrards Cross, 1977. (33)

18. Kennedy, Patrick, *The Fireside Stories,* M'Glashan and Gill, Dublin, 1870. (142)

19. Lenihan, Eddie, *Long Ago by Shannonside,* Mercier Press, Dublin, undated. (87)

20. Gregory, A., *Visions and Beliefs in the West of Ireland*, (1920), Colin Smythe, Gerrards Cross, 1976. (180-4)

21. Mac Manus, 1959/1973, op. cit. (104)

22. Ibid. (101)

23. Evans Wentz, 1911/1977, op. cit. (38)

24. Irish Folklore Commission, Vol.36 (197-200)

25. Mac Manus, 1959/1973, op. cit. (103)

26. Briggs, 1959, op. cit. (117)

27. Pocs, Eva, *Between the Living and the Dead*, (1977), Central European University Press, Budapest, 1999. (50)

28. Evans Wentz, 1911/1977, op. cit. (194)

29. Ibid. (218)

30. Cited in Olding, Frank, "Fairy Lore in 18th-Century Monmouthshire", *3rd Stone*, no. 31, 1998. (19-22)

31. Keightley, 1892/1981, op. cit. (520)

32. Mac Manus, 1959/1973, op. cit. (45-6)

33. Evans Wentz, 1911/1977, op. cit. (230-1)

34. Spindler, Konrad, *The Man in the Ice*, (1993), Phoenix, London, 1995.

35. See, for example, Katsusuke Serizawa's *Tsubo*, Japan Publications, Tokyo, 1976.

36. Taylor, Tim, "Gundestrup Cauldron", in Fagan, Brian M., (ed.), *The Oxford Companion to Archaeology*, Oxford University Press, Oxford, 1996. (269)

37. Devereux, Paul, *Mysterious Ancient* America, Vega, London, 2002. (22-3)

38. Bowen Hamer, W., *Radnorshire in History, Topography, and Romance*, 1914.

39. Nebesky-Wojkowitz, Rene de, *Oracles and Demons of Tibet*, Mouton, Holland, 1953.

Chapter Four

1. Various titles in which Paul Devereux explores these features more comprehensively include: *Shamanism and the Mystery Lines*, (1992), Quantum, Slough, 2001; *The Long Trip*, Penguin Arkana, New York, 1997; *The Sacred Place*, Cassell, London, 2000; *Haunted Land*, Piatkus, London, 2001; *Mysterious Ancient America*, Vega, London, 2002.

2. Denevan, William M., "Prehistoric roads and causeways of lowland tropical America", in Trombold, Charles D., (ed.), *Ancient Road Networks and Settlement Hierarchies in the New World*, Cambridge University Press, Cambridge, 1991.

3. Folan, William, "Sacbes of the northern Maya", in ibid.

4. Sample, L., *Trade and trails in aboriginal California*, Reports of the University of California Archaeological Survey 8, 1950.

5. Barrett, S.A. and Gifford, E.W., "Miwok material culture", in *Bulletin of the Public Museum of the City of Milwauke*, 1933.

6. Robertson, Benjamin P., "Other New World Roads and Trails", in Kincaid, Chris, (ed.), *Chaco Roads Project Phase 1,* Department of the Interior, Bureau of Land Management, Alberquerque, 1983. (2-2)

7. William Byers, cited in ibid.

8. Sever, Thomas, unpublished dissertation.

9. Lepper, Bradley T, "Tracking Ohio's Great Hopewell Road", in *Archaeology,* November/December, 1995.

10. Hylsop, John, "Observations about research on prehistoric roads in South America", in Trombold, Charles D., (ed.), *Ancient Road Networks and Settlement Hierarchies in the New World,* Cambridge University Press, Cambridge, 1991. (29-30)

11. Trombold, Charles, in ibid. (5)

12. Devereux, Paul, *Mysterious Ancient America,* Vega, London, 2002. (156)

13. Hodder, Ian, *The Domestication of Europe,* Blackwell, Oxford, 1990. (119)

14. Friedel, David, Scheie, Linda, and Parker, Joy, *Maya Cosmos,* William Morrow, New York, 1993.

15. For a full account of this whole aspect of shamanism, see Paul Devereux's *The Long Trip,* Penguin Arkana, New York, 1997.

16. Werlhof, Jay von, *Spirits of the Earth,* Imperial Valley College Museum, El Centro, 1987.

17. Dobkin de Rios, Marlene, "Plant Hallucinogens, Out-of-Body Experiences and New World Monumental Earthworks", in Du Toit, Brian, (ed.), *Drugs, Rituals and Altered States of Consciousness,* A.A. Balkema, Rotterdam, 1977.

18. Alan Ereira, personal communication.

19. Spier, Leslie, *Yuman Tribes of the Gila River,* (1933), Dover Publications, New York, 1978.

20. Devereux, 2002, op. cit. (160)

Chapter Five

1. Ucko, P.J, Hunter, M., Clark, A.J., and David, A., *Avebury Reconsidered,* Unwin Hyman, London, 1990.

2. Devereux, Paul, *Symbolic Landscapes,* Gothic Image, Glastonbury, 1992.

3. Pennick, Nigel, and Devereux, Paul, *Lines on the Landscape,* Robert Hale, London, 1989.

4. Devereux, Paul, *The Sacred Place,* Cassell, London, 2000.

5. Pennick and Devereux, 1989, op. cit.

6. Barclay, A., and Hey, G., "Cattle, cursus monuments and the river: the development of ritual and domestic landscapes in the Upper Thames Valley", in Barclay, A., and Harding, J., (eds.), *Pathways and Ceremonies,* Oxbow Books, Oxford, 1999.

7. Johnston, R., "An empty path? Processions, memories, and the Dorset Cursus", in ibid.

8. Caciola, Nancy, "Wraiths, Revenants and Ritual in Medieval Culture", in *Past and Present,* no. 152, 1996.

PART TWO (SAMPLER)

BRITAIN

1. Courtney, M.A., *Folklore and Legends of Cornwall*, (1890), Cornwall Books, 1989 edition. (207)

2. A.K. Hamilton, cited in Hawkes, Gabrielle, and Henderson-Smith, Tom, "Coffin Lines – and a Cornish Spirit Path?" in *The Ley Hunter*, no. 117, 1992.

3. Extant oral lore recorded directly by Hawkes and Henderson-Smith, ibid.

4. This could be by default if the churches themselves often occupied prehistoric sites of sanctity, as could well be the case in this ancient landscape.

5. Weatherhill, Craig, "The Zennor Churchway", in *The Ley Hunter*, no. 118, 1993.

6. Ibid.

7. Sullivan, Danny, "The Fairy Steps", in *The Ley Hunter*, no. 133, and in *Ley Lines*, Piatkus, London, 1999.

8. Dugdale, Graham, *Walks in Mysterious South Lakeland*, Sigma Leisure, Wilmslow, 1997.

9. John Drinkwater, personal communication.

10. Darwen, Norman, "A Cumbrian Corpse Path", *The Ley Hunter* no.127, 1997.

11. Brown, Theo, *Devon Ghosts*, Jarrold, Norwich, 1982. (98)

12. Devereux, Paul, *Haunted Land*, Piatkus, London, 2001.

13. Brown, Theo, *Devon Ghosts*, Jarrold, Norwich, 1982. (120)

14. St. Leger-Gordon, Ruth E., *The Witchcraft and Folklore of Dartmoor* (1965), EP Publishing, East Ardsley, 1973. (31)

15. Hemery, Eric, *Walking Dartmoor's Ancient Tracks*, Robert Hale, London, 1986. (230)

16. A contact for further information as given on "The Lych Path Walk" website is Brian Cole on 01884 32582.

17. Hemery, 1986, op. cit. (241)

18. Barber, Chips, *Widecombe in the Moor-A Visitor's Guide*, Obelisk Publications, Pinhoe, 1996.

19. Brown, Theo, "Tom Pearce's Grey Mare: A Boundary Image", in Hilda Ellis Davidson (ed.), *Boundaries and Thresholds*, The Katharine Briggs Club, 1993.

20. Ibid.

21. Biggam, C.P., *Grey in Old English*, Runetree Press, London, 1998.

22. Menefee, Samuel Pyeatt, "Dead Reckoning: the Church Porch Watch in British Society", in Davidson, Hilda Ellis, (ed.), *The Seer in Celtic and Other Traditions*, John Donald, Edinburgh, 1989.

23. Harte, Jeremy, "Haunted Roads", in *The Ley Hunter*, no.21, 1994. (5)

24. Devereux, Paul, and Thomson, Ian, *The Ley Hunter's Companion*, Thames & Hudson, London, 1979. (207)

25. The analysis, conducted in 1978 by Robert Forrest, yielded significance at the one-percent level.

26. Main, Laurence, "A Coffin Path on the Oxfordshire Way", in *The Ley Hunter*, no. 130, 1998.

27. Roberts, Tony, "The Monk's Ford Ley", in *The Ley Hunter*, no. 20, 1971.

28. Ibid.

29. Coles, Bryony and John, *Sweet Track to Glastonbury*, Thames & Hudson, London, 1986. (43)

30. Bloom, J. Harvey, *Folk Lore in Shakespeare Land*, (1930), EP Publishing, East Ardsley, 1976. (48-49)

31. Woodward, Alfred, *Memories of Brailes*, Peter Drinkwater, Shipston-on-Stour, 1988.

32. Alfred Woodward, personal communication.

33. Hoggard, Brian, "Dead Sunny", in *The Ley Hunter*, no. 125, 1996. (16)

34. Devereux, Paul, *The Sacred Place*, Cassell, London, 2000. (154-155)

35. Bloom, 1930/1976, op. cit.

36. Sullivan, Jo, "Burial Lane at Feckenham", in *The Ley Hunter*, no.130, 1998. See also Sullivan, Danny, 1999, op. cit.

37. Swallow, Bob, "On the Pennine Way", in *The Dalesman*, October, 1993.

38. Ford, Joseph, *Some Reminiscences and Folk Lore of Danby Parish and District*, Home & Son, Whitby, 1953.

39. Atkinson, J.C., *Forty Years in a Moorland Parish*, Macmillan, London, 1891.

40. Ford, 1953, op. cit.

41. Wysocki, Michael, "Scotland's Serpent Mound", in *The Ley Hunter*, no. 94, 1982.

42. Smith, Jill, "The 'Hag' Mountain Funeral Path on South Harris", in *The Ley Hunter*, no. 123, 1995.

43. Ibid.

44. Cited in Olding, Frank, "Fairy Lore in 18th-century Monmouthshire", in *3rd Stone*, no.31, 1998.

45. Ibid., and personal communication.

46. Jones, Edmund, *A Geographical, Historical, and Religious Account of the Parish of Aberystruth*, 1779, cited in Olding, 1998, op. cit.

47. Jones, 1779, in ibid.

48. Frank Olding, personal communication.

49. Olding, 1998, op. cit., and personal communication.

50. Dutton, R.J. A., *Hidden Highways of North Wales*, Gordon Emery, Chester, 1997. (35)

51. Main, Laurence, "A North Welsh Corpse Road", in *The Ley Hunter*, no. 132, 1998, and Main, Laurence, *The Spirit Paths of Wales*, Cicerone Press, Milnthorpe, 2000. (30-33)

52. Dutton, 1997, op. cit.

53. Esgairadda (marked and named on the map) is close to Troed-y-Rhiw and was a

ruin for a considerable period, but has now been refurbished.

54. Main, Laurence, and Perrott, Morag, *Welsh Walks: Dolgellau and the Cambrian Coast*, Sigma, Wilmslow, 1992, and also personal communication.

GERMANY

1. Magin, Ulrich, "An Assortment of Landscape Lines in Germany Real and Imagined", in *The Ley Hunter*, no. 133, 1999.

2. Palmer, John, "A Rothenburg Death Road", in *The Ley Hunter*, no. 126, 1997.

3. Magin, Ulrich, "The Old Straight Track on Dragon Mountain", in *The Ley Hunter*, no. 117, 1992.

4. Palmer, John, "Crossing the Border – The Meinweg Corpse Road", in *The Ley Hunter*, no. 131, 1998.

IRELAND

1. This site is on private land and there is no automatic right of way. If visited at all, it would be best to ask permission and directions – during fieldwork I was kindly shown an otherwise unknowable route to the cashel by local people.

2. Bob Curran, personal communication. (Curran's books include: *Banshees, Beasts and Brides from the Sea: Irish tales of the Supernatural* [1996], *A Field Guide to Irish Fairies* [1997], and *Complete Guide to Celtic Mythology* [2000].)

3. "Devereux" being one of those . . .

4. Lysaght, Patricia, *A Pocket Book of the Banshee*, O'Brien Press, Dublin, 1998. (26)

5. Lenihan, Eddie, "Otherworldly Clare", a six-part series published in the *Journal* of the Clare Archaeological & Historical Society between 1985-1990. Also personal communication.

6. Ryan, Meda, *Biddy Early – The Wise Woman of Clare*, (1978), Mercier Press, Dublin, 1991, (79-80).

7. Ibid.

8. Puhvel, Martin, *The Crossroads in Folklore and Myth*, American University Studies, Peter Lang, New York, 1989; see also Paul Devereux's *Haunted Land*, Piatkus, London, 2001.

9. Some dark hour between 9-11 August, 2002.

10. Taken from the poem "Portrait With Chainsaw" in Eddie Lenihan's book of poetry, *A Loss of Face and Other Poems*, Inchicronan Press, 1984.

11. The efforts of the St. Colman's Heritage Association in Conahy, County Kilkenny, is a noteworthy example of this. It has researched numerous Mass paths leading to churches in Conahy and elsewhere, and gives information concerning them on its website. This can be accessed on the World Wide Web by reaching the Local Ireland website and keying in "Conahy" in the Search window.

12. On the map the positioning of the church and the motte is erroneously reversed.

NETHERLANDS

1. Palmer, John, "Lykwei to Harich" in *The Ley Hunter,* no. 131, 1998.

2. Palmer, John, "Death Roads in Holland", in *The Ley Hunter,* no. 126, 1997.

3. Palmer, John, "The Deathroads of Holland", in *The Ley Hunter,* no. 109, 1989.

AUSTRALIA

1. Those who want a much more complete account than can be given here should consult: Mountford, Charles P., *Winbaraku and the Myth of Jarapiri,* Rigby, Adelaide, 1968.

2. Ibid.

3. Ibid.

4. Meggitt, M.J., *Gadjari Among the Walbiri Aborigines of Central Australia,* The *Oceania* Monographs, No. 14, University of Sydney, Sydney, 1966.

5. Ibid. (7)

6. Ibid. (9)

7. Ibid. (16)

8. Lorraine Maafi-Williams, personal communication.

COSTARICA

1. Sheets, Payson, and Sever, Thomas L., "Prehistoric footpaths in Costa Rica: transportation and communication in a tropical rainforest", in Trombold, C. (ed.), *Ancient Road Networks and Settlement Hierarchies in the New World,* Cambridge University Press, Cambridge, 1991.

2. Ibid.

MEXICO

1. Folan, William J., "Sacbes of the Northern Maya", in Trombold, C. (ed.), *Ancient Road Networks and Settlement Hierarchies in the New World,* Cambridge University Press, Cambridge, 1991.

2. Gann, Thomas, *Mystery Cities of the Maya,* Duckworth, London, 1925.

3. Trombold, Charles D., "Causeways in the context of strategic planning in the La Quemada region, Zacatecas, Mexico", in Trombold, (ed.), 1991, op. cit.

UNITED STATES

1. Rozendal, Michael, "Palm Springs and the Desert", in *California '96,* Berkeley Guides, Fodor, New York, 1995, (422).

2. David Whitley, personal communication.

3. Werlhof, Jay von, *Spirits of the Earth,* Imperial Valley College Museum, El Centro,

1987, (29).

4. Because these sites are both subtle and exceedingly fragile they can inadvertently be damaged by an untrained visitor's inability to recognise them and accidentally stumbling through them, quite apart from the risk of deliberate vandalism (which is, alas, all too prevalent at ancient sites in America, and has actually occurred at this very site at some point in the last twenty years, as was discovered during the fieldwork for this Sampler). Further, the sites are so delicate they could not withstand too many people visiting them.

For any or all of these reasons I trust the reader will forgive me if I do not specify the exact location of this site, and hope the text and visual descriptions given will be sufficient to give an idea of this kind of feature – this entry is for the purposes of information, which is in any case one of the main functions of the Sampler. On the other hand, Death Valley in itself is well worth visiting in its own right! There is prehistoric rock art in the valley, as well as in the Coso range to the west across the Panamint Valley. This rock art is largely shamanic and belongs to the same peoples who made the ground markings and relates to the same purposes. The best – if not the only – detailed guide to the rock art of the area is David Whitley's excellent *A Guide to Rock Art Sites*, Mountain Press, Missoula, 1996.

5.Werlhof, 1987, op. cit. (13)

6. Hurst, Winston, Severance, Owen, and Davidson, Dale, "Uncle Albert's Ancient Roads", in *Blue Mountain Shadows*, vol. 12, Summer, 1993.

7. Sever, Thomas, unpublished dissertation.

8. Frazier, Kendrick, *People ofChaco*, Norton, New York, 1986. (111)

9. Ibid.

APPENDIX
About Grid References

In the British and Irish entries in the Sampler, letter-and-number combinations are given after specific locations. These are grid references, which provide a precise location on the appropriate Ordnance Survey map.

Each Ordnance Survey map sheet is covered by a grid of vertical and horizontal lines. The vertical lines are called Eastings because they "march" eastwards, i.e. their numbers in the top and bottom margins of the map sheet increase toward the right of the map sheet. The horizontal grid lines are called **Northings** because their numbers advance from bottom to top of the map sheet.

To give the grid reference of a specific point on, say, a 1:50,000-scale (1¼-inch-to-the-mile) map, the two-figure number of the Easting (vertical line) forming the west or left-hand edge of the grid square it is in is given first, then the number of tenths the point lies eastwards (right) of that line. These three figures are followed by the two numbers of the Northing or horizontal line forming the bottom of the grid square the point is in, then the number of tenths the point is above (north) of that line. This gives a six-figure reference number that provides the co-ordinates of the point lying in the square. The tenths form the Easting and Northing lines can be estimated by eye, or found

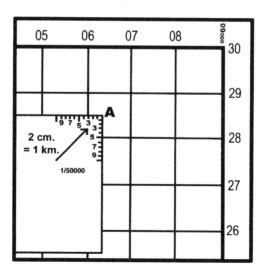

Fig. 21. Using a romer to read off a grid reference. (After Ian Thomson)

by use of a romer, which can be purchased from any map or outdoor sports shop and is illustrated in Figure 27. In that figure, the grid reference of point A is 063285 (which can also be written 063.285 or 063 285). It is essential that the Easting reference be given before that of the Northing.

In the Sampler it will be noticed that some locations are provided with an eight-figure grid reference rather than the six-figure one described here. An eight-figure reference is arrived at simply by estimating or reading off tenths of the tenths – this can only be done practically on maps of scale 1:25,000 (2½-inches-to-the-mile). (Romers have 1:25,000-scale as well as 1:50,000-scale calibrations.) I have used eight-figure references only where I feel it is helpful to give a particularly precise location of a place or feature.

The placing of prefix letters in front of the numerical grid reference ensures that the reference is unique for the whole country. If one knows which map sheet is being used these are not always essential, but is nevertheless wise to indicate them when giving a grid reference for someone else's use. The appropriate prefix letters for a given map sheet will be found in the map sheet's margin, where a summary of how to use grid references is also usually given.

It is all much simpler than it sounds!

INDEX

Figures in *italics* indicate captions.

Index

Index

Index